P9-CRT-893

Teaching Reading in the Content Areas

If Not Me, Then Who?

Teacher's Manual
2nd Edition

Rachel Billmeyer, Ph.D.
Mary Lee Barton, M.Ed.

McREL

2550 S. Parker Road, Suite 500 • Aurora, Colorado 80014

(303) 337-0990 • FAX (303) 337-3005

Teaching Reading in the Content Areas: If Not Me, Then Who?
2nd Edition
Rachel Billmeyer
Mary Lee Barton

This publication is based on work sponsored wholly, or in part, by the Office of Educational Research and Improvement, Department of Education, under Contract Number RP91002005. The content of this publication does not necessarily reflect the views of OERI or any other agency of the U.S. Government.

To purchase additional copies of this book, contact

Association for Supervision and Curriculum Development
1703 N. Beauregard St. • Alexandria, VA 22311-1714 USA
Telephone: 800-933-2723 or 703-578-9600 • Fax: 703-575-5400
Web site: http://www.ascd.org • E-mail: member@ascd.org

Discounts for bulk purchases are available.

ASCD Stock Number #397258
ISBN: 1-893476-05-7

Price: $27.95

Teaching Reading in the Content Areas:
If Not Me, Then Who?

TRAINING WORKSHOPS AVAILABLE

The McREL Institute delivers training and consultation on *Teaching Reading in the Content Areas: If Not Me, Then Who?* to teachers, reading specialists, staff developers, and administrators. The Teachers Workshop, designed for upper elementary, middle school, and high school educators, provides an overview of content area reading instruction; engages participants in applying vocabulary, reading, and discussion strategies to specific content covered in their classrooms; and offers practical suggestions on integrating these strategies into existing curricula.

The Training-of-Trainers Workshop is designed for teachers who have a background in reading or who have completed the Teachers Workshop. Participants delve more deeply into critical conceptual ideas underlying the teaching of content area reading skills; receive guidelines for facilitating adult learning; discuss training issues, questions, and concerns; share and critique training plans for teaching content area reading strategies; and discuss school-wide implementation planning.

For more information about scheduling workshops and consulting services, contact the McREL Institute at (303) 337-0990.

Table of Contents

McREL

Acknowledgements

Over the years, the authors have attended a number of workshops and received handouts that only occasionally identify the original source. Whenever possible, we have tried to acknowledge the author; if we have inadvertently included an individual's work without giving credit, please contact McREL and we will rectify this error in the next edition. Both the authors and McREL staff have used these ideas with educators in workshops, and the feedback from participants has enhanced the form in which they are presented here.

Special thanks to McREL staff who provided editing expertise for this edition, Shae Isaacs and Kevin Cooney, and to Norma Brown, who oversaw copyright permissions. We also gratefully acknowledge the efforts of Linda Button, who assisted with quality assurance review; Lyn Chambers, who contributed to the editing of this document, and Leah Dixon, who performed the desktop publishing portion of this project.

McREL

Teaching Reading in the Content Areas:

If Not Me, Then Who?

> "Learning to read is critical to a child's overall well-being. If a youngster does not learn to read in a literacy-driven society, hope for a fulfilling, productive life diminishes."
>
> G. Reid Lyon,
> Chief of the Child Development and Behavior Branch of the
> National Institute of Child Health and Human Development

Rationale

"No, I don't read much; actually, I haven't read a book all summer. I guess the only thing I read is the sports page," commented my daughter's boyfriend. Knowing that Brian is valedictorian of the senior class, I asked him about the reading involved with his assignments in school. "Oh, I read what I need to in order to get by, but nothing more. I know I should read," he admitted, "but I just don't get into it."

Brian is not an atypical student. Many students admit they don't read very much—sometimes not even the required homework. In a long-term assessment of academic progress published in 1997, the National Assessment of Educational Progress (NAEP) found that nearly half of the 9-, 13-, and 17-year-old students they surveyed reported reading 10 pages or less each day, including pages read in school and for homework! The same report revealed, however, that 36 percent of the 9-year olds, 48 percent of the 13-year-olds and 39 percent of the 17-year-olds did find time to watch 3 to 5 hours of television per day (National Center for Education Statistics, 1997).

The fact that students don't read very much may not come as a surprise to classroom teachers; however, adults are not reading, either. Some aren't reading because they lack reading skills. An alarming percentage of our adult population—from 15 to 30 percent—have such poor reading skills that they have difficulty reading common print material: news articles, report cards, coupons, recipes, even the directions on prescription medicine bottles (Stedman and Kaestle, 1991; cf., Barton, 1997).

Others who can read are simply choosing not to do so. According to Dr. Bernice Cullinan of New York University, approximately 80 percent of the books in this country are read by about 10 percent of the people (Cullinan, 1987). Weekday and Sunday newspaper readership has declined in the past several decades, suggesting that people are choosing to get their news from nonprint media.

Of major concern is that many of our preservice teachers actually dislike reading and avoid it whenever possible. A study conducted by two Kent State University education professors found that students enrolled in children's literature courses entered with a very negative attitude toward reading in general and, more specifically, toward literature. In fact, more than one-quarter potential teachers acknowledged a "lifelong discomfort with print," and many admitted that they made it through literature courses primarily by relying on Cliff Notes, book jackets, or anything that would allow them to get by (Mann and Misheff, 1987). The evidence seems clear; people aren't choosing to read, and if they must read for work or school, they don't enjoy it. And yet, people become good readers only by reading a lot!

The difficulties students have with school reading assignments are caused by a variety of skill-related issues. Many students have trouble understanding an author's ideas because they haven't learned how to mentally organize those ideas as they read. Or, they have not had much experience with the topic and don't know how to make meaningful and personal connections to new ideas while reading. Many simply label the assignment as "too hard" or "boring" because they lack effective reading and self-regulation skills needed to persevere and succeed.

Because students often resist classroom reading assignments, teachers may at times lose confidence in using the textbook. Rather than struggle with unmotivated students, a teacher may resort to telling the class what they need to know rather than have them read it. Or, teachers may rely on other media to provide the instruction, even though they are aware that significant portions of the curriculum need to be print-based, and that students need to develop and practice effective reading skills in order to survive in a society that is calling for even higher literacy standards.

Content area teachers know that reading is a complex process, and they often struggle with the following questions:

- What are the specific skills or knowledge that students need in order to read effectively?

- What learning environment promotes effective reading and learning?

McREL

- What strategies might I use with my students that will help them become more effective readers and independent learners?

The information in this manual is designed to help teachers answer these questions.

This manual is intended to be a resource to assist teachers in expanding and refining their repertoire of teaching strategies. It can also serve as a guide for instructional planning and decision making when teaching reading in the content areas. It is not intended to prescribe a particular style of teaching – one "best" method or model. Rather, it is meant to be a resource for teachers as they consider their curriculum objectives, the nature and needs of their students, and their personal teaching styles.

There are many aspects to consider when teaching reading in the content areas. As educators, we need to understand the big picture about learning, the premises that guide the teaching of reading in content areas, the vast array of reading strategies available, and then how to use this information to impact all learners. The following four major areas comprise the contents of this publication:

1. We examine the **three interactive elements** of the reading process that influence comprehension: what the reader brings to the situation; the learning climate; and the characteristics of the written text, or the text features.

2. **Strategies:** We have compiled 40 popular teaching strategies that can be adapted for students from elementary through high school and that are appropriate for students in all content areas.

3. **Strategic teaching:** As a decision maker, the teacher must consciously plan for teaching reading in all content areas, and this section shares a framework for instructional planning.

4. **Six assumptions about learning:** The research on learning serves as the foundation for this publication, and so the critical implications for instruction are discussed. This section can serve as the introduction or as the conclusion to this publication. Big-picture thinkers may enjoy the information up front while other readers may want an understanding of the reading process and strategies first.

These four sections are presented graphically in Figure 1 on the next page.

Teaching Reading in the Content Areas:
If Not Me, Then Who?

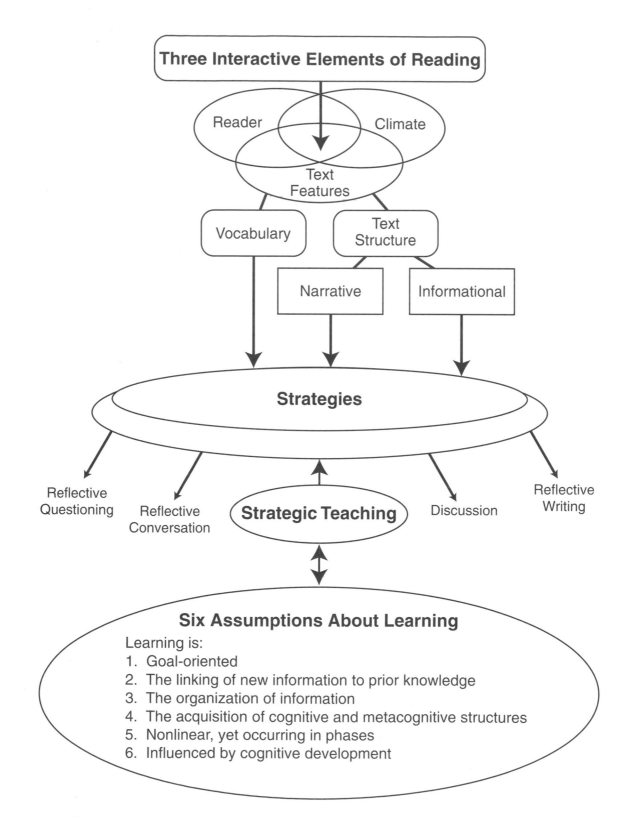

Figure 1. Model of Teaching Reading in the Content Areas

Section 1

Three Interactive Elements of Reading

> "Reading transcends the mere transmission of information: It fosters an imaginative dialogue between the text and the reader's mind that actually helps people to think."
>
> Stratford P. Sherman
> Author of "America Won't Win Till It Reads More"

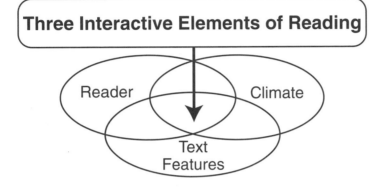

Introduction

At its most basic, teaching reading in the content areas is helping learners to make connections between what they already know and "new" information presented in the text. As students make these connections, they create meaning; they comprehend what they are reading. Teaching reading in the content areas, therefore, is not so much about teaching students basic reading skills as it is about teaching students how to use reading as a tool for thinking and learning. Until recently, learning was thought to be a passive activity: teachers poured their knowledge into the receptive minds of students. Reading was thought to be passive as well. The words of the text contained meaning; reading simply entailed decoding the words on the page. Recent research indicates, however, that learning and reading are active processes. Readers construct meaning as they read. Effective readers are strategic. They make predictions, organize information, and interact with the text. They evaluate the ideas they are reading about in light of what they already know. They monitor their comprehension, and know when

1

and how to modify their reading behaviors when they have problems understanding what they read. (See Figure 2).

	Traditional Views	**New Definition of Reading**
Research Base	Behaviorism	Cognitive sciences
Goals of Reading	Mastery of isolated facts and skills	Constructing meaning and self-regulated learning
Reading as Process	Mechanically decoding words; memorizing by rote	An interaction among the reader, the text, and the context
Learner Role/Metaphor	Passive; vessel receiving knowledge from external sources	Active; strategic reader, effective strategy user, cognitive apprentice

<u>Figure 2.</u> **Historical view of reading**

Three elements working interactively determine the meaning a reader constructs from a text. They are the **reader,** and what she brings to the situation; the learning **climate,** or the environment in which the reading occurs; and the **text features,** or specific characteristics of the written text. To fully understand how these three elements affect the reading process, a short summary of the findings from cognitive science is helpful.

Research from cognitive science identifies five premises that are basic to the teaching of content area reading skills:

1. The meaning of a text is not contained in the words on the page. Instead, the reader **constructs** meaning by making what she thinks is a logical, sensible connection between the new information she reads and what she already knows about the topic. Researchers believe that what we know is stored in knowledge frameworks called "schemata." Learners draw on these schemata to make inferences and predictions, organize and reflect on new information, and elaborate on it (Vacca and Vacca, 1993). When learners are confronted with "new" information, they try to make sense of it by seeing how it fits with what they already know. In other words, they try to match this new information with existing schema (singular of

schemata) so that it can be understood. To illustrate, read the paragraph below and fill in the missing words:

The questions that p_____ face as they raise ch_____ from in_____ to adult life are not easy to an_____. Both fa_____ and m_____ can become concerned when health problems such as co_____ arise any time after the e_____ stage to later life. Experts recommend that young ch_____ should have plenty of s_____ and nutritious food for healthy growth. B_____ and g_____ should not share the same b_____ or even sleep in the same r_____. They may be afraid of the d_____.

How did you do? (Check your answers on page 4.)

This passage illustrates that deriving meaning is not simply a matter of reading the words on the page. In order to comprehend, the reader selects a schema that seems appropriate and connects it with the new information, filling in any gaps so that the text makes sense. Because no two students bring the same background and experience to class, no two students will comprehend a text passage in the same way.

2. Closely related to schema theory is the role **prior knowledge** plays in learning. According to Vacca and Vacca (1993), "the single most important variable in learning with texts is a reader's prior knowledge" (p.13). Research (Anthony and Raphael, 1989) and common sense tell us that the more a reader brings to the text in terms of knowledge and skills, the more he will learn and remember from what he reads.

> "The meaning of things lies not in the things themselves but in our attitude toward them."
>
> Saint-Exupéry,
> *The Wisdom of the Sands (1948)*

3. How well a reader comprehends a text is also dependent on **metacognition:** his ability to think about and to control his thinking process before, during, and after reading. Students who have learned metacognitive skills can plan and monitor their comprehension, adapting and modifying their reading accordingly. Ineffective readers often are unaware that there is anything they should be doing while reading except moving

their eyes across the page. They have never been taught that they should think about what they are reading, create mental pictures, and ask questions (e.g., "Do I understand this? What do I need to do to fix things if I don't understand? Do I get the author's point? How does it fit with what I already know? What do I think the author will discuss next?") Low-achieving students, in particular, need to be taught how to monitor their understanding and to select and use appropriate "fix-up" strategies when needed (Pogrow, 1993; Caverly, Manderville and Nicholson, 1995).

4. Reading and writing are integrally related. Laflamme (1997) asserts that "reading and writing are two analogous and complementary processes" because both involve generating ideas, organizing them into a logical order, "drafting" them a number of times until they make sense, and then revising them as needed. The connection between reading and writing is also evident in research, which has shown that students who are taught how to write and edit different forms of expository text improve their comprehension of their content textbooks (Raphael, Kirschner and Englert, 1988).

5. Learning increases when students collaborate in the learning process. Quite simply, learning is a socially interactive process (Vygotsky, 1978). Students learn by interacting with others in the classroom, when they feel free to generate questions, and discuss their ideas freely with the teacher and one another. Dialogue can spark new ideas. Moreover, the process of verbalizing one's understanding of an idea or concept deepens understanding and also offers listeners an opportunity to compare their thinking to what is said. Finally, as students have opportunities to instruct one another, they assume more responsibility for their own learning and that of their fellow students.

These premises have implications not only for the learner but also for the content area teacher who wants to plan instruction that helps students improve their reading comprehension and learning.

Notes

Check Your Answers
The questions that poultrymen face as they raise chickens from incubation to adult life are not easy to answer. Both farmers and merchants can become concerned when health problems such as coccidiosis arise any time after the egg stage to later life. Experts recommend that young chicks should have plenty of sunshine and nutritious food for healthy growth. Banties and geese should not share the same barnyard or even sleep in the same roost. They may be afraid of the dark.

Adapted from Madeline Hunter

McREL

Specifically, teachers can focus their planning around the interaction of these key elements:

1. The reader: what the reader brings to the learning experience.

2. The climate: the learning context or environment.

3. The text features: the characteristics of the written text.

Embedded within each of these elements are features that affect which strategies may be most effective for a particular reader at different times during the learning process. Therefore, we will examine each element separately and look at the implications each has for strategy selection and use.

The Role of the Reader

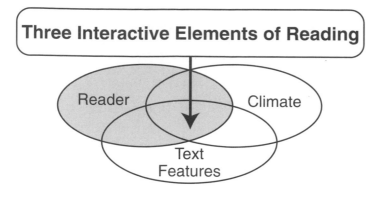

"No, I didn't finish reading the homework. It was way too hard. I mean, I have no clue about chromosomes, or whatever the chapter was about. How can you expect me to read the chapter if it doesn't make any sense?"

"'What did we read yesterday?' Well... uh... I think it was something about... Bosnia, no, wait... um... maybe it was Botswana? I don't know... it was about some foreign country that started with a B. Why do we have to know that stuff anyway? We'll never need it."

"But I did read the story. I just don't remember it, that's all. I never do. I can read something three times and still not remember what I read."

Do these comments sound familiar? Students who struggle with reading often give up on reading and sometimes lose confidence in themselves as students. To them, reading comprehension is something of a mystery. They think that comprehension just happens, or ought to, if one can decode the words on the page. When they aren't successful at comprehending what they read, they blame the text, themselves, even their teacher. These students are unaware that comprehension requires more than simple decoding. They haven't been taught that readers have an active role to play while reading. Effective readers interact with the author of the text while they read, work to make sense of the text and how it aligns with what they already know, and apply strategies to stay on task.

They have learned that comprehension is something that really "takes place behind the eyes" (Vacca and Vacca, p. 16).

Certainly the ability to decode a word is important; however, the reader's role extends beyond using basic reading skills to two key inner resources: (1) **prior knowledge** and (2) **mental disposition**, or the reader's affective response to reading content area text (Frager, 1993).

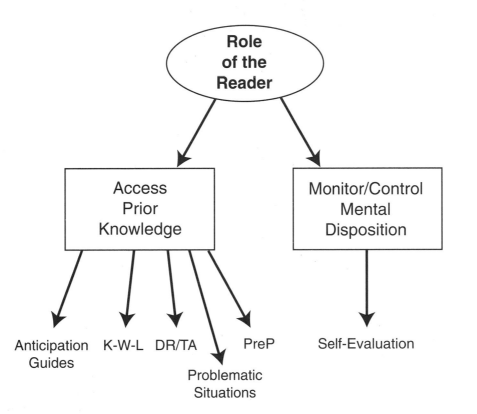

Prior Knowledge

As noted earlier, prior knowledge is the content knowledge and personal experiences the reader brings to the learning task. Teachers know that students bring a wide range of background knowledge and experiences to class. The same class may contain students whose families are highly educated and encourage reading of all kinds, students whose experience of the world is limited to what they see on TV, and students for whom English is a second—or even a third—language. Faced with this mix of backgrounds, effective teachers help students prepare for reading as much as possible by incorporating prereading strategies that activate and assess learners'

prior knowledge. Pulling forward that knowledge gives readers a structure on which to attach new learnings.

Teachers can help students to activate their prior knowledge in a variety of ways: brainstorming, asking questions, discussing the topic, and providing analogies. This manual contains five additional strategies teachers can use to help students recall what they know:

- K-W-L (What I Know, Want to Know, and Learned)
- DR/TA (Directed Reading/Thinking Activity)
- PreP (Prereading Plan)
- Anticipation Guides
- Problematic Situations

These can be found in the informational text strategies at the end of this manual.

Even before introducing these strategies, the teacher should consider discussing the benefits of strategy use. We know that students are more motivated to learn when they see the value in the learning. Consequently, it's helpful to point out that studies have been conducted on the benefits of strategy use; these have shown that all students can benefit from using reading strategies, especially those who have had trouble in the past with reading (Palincsar and Brown, 1984; cf. Barton, 1997).

Strategies that help readers "take out and dust off" prior knowledge before reading directly affect learning. Readers who have that information available can make more connections and learn more while they read. Those readers whose prior knowledge is accessible and well-developed remember more from their reading than readers whose prior knowledge of the topic is limited (Anthony and Raphael, 1989).

Using these prereading strategies in class benefits not just the students whose prior knowledge is well-developed, however.

McREL

Students whose backgrounds are more limited can learn from their more experienced peers. In effect, the students teach one another as they engage in these strategies.

Incorporating strategies to access prior knowledge can yield useful information for teachers, as well. As students express what they already know, teachers can determine which students might need a more thorough grounding in a topic before reading. Additionally, these prereading strategies can reveal if the information students "know" is accurate. Studies show that readers who have misperceptions about a topic often overlook, misinterpret, or don't remember text information that disagrees with their background information, however incorrect that might be (Anderson and Smith, 1984; cf. Barton, 1997). Using prereading strategies can expose any misperceptions, and teachers can correct these before assigning text.

The ultimate goal of strategy instruction is independence. We want students to recognize which strategies work well for them, and we want them to practice those strategies to the point where they will use them naturally when reading on their own. Consequently, anything teachers can do to foster this independence is beneficial. For example, when explaining the impact that prior knowledge has on learning, teachers might also discuss with students how one's prior experience can influence his perceptions and judgment. Literature, history, current events, even television programs contain a wealth of illustrations, both comic and tragic, of how people's past experiences color the way they view the world. Students can reflect on times when their own background and experience caused them to misjudge another person, group, or situation. When students recognize that perceptions are not fact, and that schema can be revised as we learn new information, they also will see that they have the power to control what they think and what they learn.

McREL

Mental Disposition

A second component in the reader's role in comprehending text is his mental disposition, or affective response toward reading. The reader's mental disposition encompasses such things as:

- how motivated he is to do what is required;

- how confident he feels about his ability to succeed at reading;

- how interested he is in actively pursuing meaning while reading;

- how he feels about what he is reading; and

- how much new learning he wants to integrate into his current schema (Frager, 1993).

Our mental habits influence everything we do. For example, if a reader has a poor attitude toward reading because she thinks she reads poorly and can't understand unfamiliar text, chances are that this attitude will become a self-fulfilling prophecy: in continuing to maintain that attitude, she will approach difficult text reluctantly, give up easily if she meets any obstacles, and therefore, not understand what she was assigned to read.

Even skilled readers can encounter problems if they haven't developed effective mental habits. For example, an individual might possess knowledge and skill in reading fiction, but run into difficulty reading a computer manual. He may not be skilled at or enjoy reading technical material; in this case, he needs to apply the mental habits of maintaining an open mind, pushing the limits of his knowledge and abilities, and persevering.

These mental habits are referred to as "intelligent behaviors" (Costa, 1991), or "habits of mind" (Marzano, Pickering, Arredondo, Blackburn, Brandt, Moffett, Paynter, Pollack, and Whisler, 1997). Quite simply, these are life skills that can help learners not only in school but throughout their lives. Productive mental dispositions outlined by Marzano and Pickering et al. (1997), Costa (1991), Perkins (1993), and Paul (1990) include:

McREL

- being open-minded and flexible about ideas and solutions;

- being aware of your own thinking, behaviors, and feelings;

- being accurate and seeking accuracy;

- being clear and seeking clarity;

- being able to monitor and control your behavior, learning, and work;

- planning appropriately;

- responding appropriately to feedback;

- identifying and using necessary resources; and

- restraining impulsivity.

How can we help students acquire these habits? First, explain what these behaviors are and that they enhance learning; lower-achieving students may not realize that their attitude, mental habits, and frame of mind affect their learning, or that they have the power to regulate these feelings, attitudes, and behaviors. Second, provide clear examples for students: model productive habits of mind, discuss real world examples that appear in the news or other media, and reinforce their use in class. Learners who practice these behaviors become self-directed learners who are aware of their mental disposition, monitor it, and modify it as needed.

In summary, effective readers know that comprehension is not something that just happens. Readers have a role in the reading process. Ideal readers:

- understand that activating prior knowledge of the topic will help them understand and remember more of what they read;

- actively pursue meaning;

- interact with the text, asking questions like "What is this about? How does it fit with what I already know? What point is the author trying to make? How do I feel about what the author is saying?"

- monitor their attitude, and know how to modify their mental habits when difficulties arise.

The Role of Climate

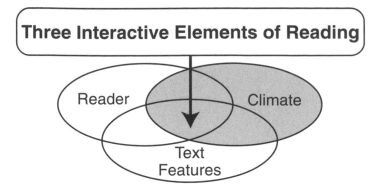

Three Interactive Elements of Reading

Reader   Climate

Text Features

Picture the following scenario: you are returning from a conference on comprehensive school reform and have a binder full of conference material you need to read. You are expected to give a report to your superintendent summarizing the conference materials an hour after you land. You are nervous about air travel, and the captain has just announced that the turbulence you feel will be getting worse. Everyone is to remain in their seats for the duration of the flight, seatbelts tightly fastened. The young mother sitting next to you is trying vainly to soothe her 10-month-old baby, who is squalling and pulling at his ear; the woman apologizes for the noise, explaining that the baby has an ear infection.

How well would you be able to focus on reading?

This scenario illustrates the role that climate can play in reading comprehension. Clearly, the environment in which reading occurs influences learning. In this manual, we use the term *climate* to refer to physical conditions, such as temperature or noise level in the area, and also affective dimensions, such as how safe the reader feels, how competent, even how he feels about others around him.

While teachers have little control over the environment in which students do their homework, they are able to create an environment in their classrooms that enhances learning. Research suggests that students learn best in a pleasant, friendly climate where they

- feel accepted by their teachers and their peers;

- feel a sense of safety and order because academic expectations, instructions, and the purpose for assignments are clear;

- feel confident in their ability to complete tasks successfully; and

- see the value in the learning activities

(Marzano and Pickering et al., 1997; McCombs and Barton, 1998).

Acceptance

Teachers can create a climate of acceptance in a number of ways. Students report feeling accepted when their teachers listen to them and respect their opinions. Teachers communicate acceptance when they are interested not only in how students perform in class but also in their extracurricular activities. Calling students by their preferred name, making eye contact, planning varied activities that address different learning styles and that capitalize on individual differences, encouraging even the unassertive students to participate in class discussion—all of these help students feel like they matter.

Even a simple, sincere gesture can help students feel connected to their teacher and school. For instance, a Kansas middle school teacher reported she made a point of standing at the classroom door at the end of class every day. As each student left the room, she would either shake his hand or give him a "high five." She didn't realize the impact this had on her students until she was absent one day. When she returned, students complained that her substitute didn't follow her end-of-class routine. On a whim, the teacher subsequently made a photocopy of her hand and left it in her "sub" folder with instructions to tape it to the classroom door frame on days she was out of the building. Substitutes reported in some amazement that students would "high five" the hand print as they left the classroom.

Students are more receptive to learning if they feel accepted by their classmates as well as their teacher. Collaborative learning activities call for teamwork and can be an excellent means for students to

McREL

learn about one another's strengths, aptitudes, and personalities. Another strategy that teachers have said students respond well to is "home court advantage." Students are asked to view their classroom as a basketball court and class time as a home game. In this analogy, students are teammates working together to achieve a common goal: succeeding in class. Therefore, the classroom atmosphere should be just as supportive as that of a home court.

Safety and Order

Naturally, individuals need to feel safe from physical harm in order to be receptive to learning. Across the nation, teachers, administrators, and parents are working together to introduce and enforce school-wide procedures aimed at violence prevention. Students also need to feel a sense of emotional safety—that is, that they are safe from emotional abuse. Within their individual classrooms, teachers can create a healthy climate by making it clear that any form of put-down or abusive behavior will not be tolerated.

Often, students feel open to ridicule by their classmates when asking questions about class work they don't understand. A middle school math teacher in Colorado gave us the following solution: she reserves a large table in the classroom for students who need extra help during class. At the beginning of each school year, she explains to her classes that this table is "sacred," a place where anyone can join her and receive help without worrying about what other students might say. Students quickly learn to regard this space with respect, knowing that there will be times when they need to use it. The teacher reports that at times there may be several students with her at the table, and at other times there may only be one or two; however, all of her students treat with respect those classmates who elect to be there.

A sense of order is enhanced when teachers clearly articulate classroom rules and the purposes for each reading assignment. Students should know ahead of time what they will be doing with

M℠REL

the information they read in the text; for example, will they be taking a true-false quiz, writing a summary, collaborating with others on an extended performance activity, or participating in a discussion of the material? **How** one reads a text will vary, depending on whether her purpose is to learn specific facts, to acquire a general understanding of a concept, or to interpret and evaluate the author's message. Ineffective readers do not differentiate among reading assignments. They read all textbooks in the same fashion. It is important that students learn that a reader's purpose determines which strategies he employs, the pace at which he reads, the type of mental questions he asks and answers while reading, how he monitors his comprehension, and so on.

Competence and Value

Students are more likely to learn when they feel capable of succeeding and when they see the relevance of the learning activities. Teachers can engender feelings of competence by:

- helping students develop confidence in their ability to access prior knowledge;

- filling in any gaps in necessary background knowledge prior to assigning reading;

- showing students how to "chunk up" assigned work into manageable pieces;

- acknowledging small successes as well as large ones;

- encouraging risk-taking in answering questions about what they have read; and

- validating responses, giving credit for correct aspects of an incorrect response.

Lastly, students need to see value in what they are asked to do. Although content area teachers are fascinated by their subject area, their students may not share that excitement, yet. Enthusiasm can be contagious. Explanations about what students will gain from learning content material also help to increase motivation.

The Role of Text Features

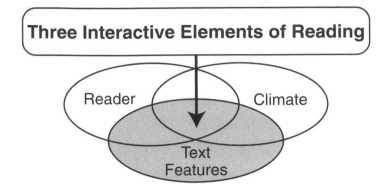

Just as facial features distinguish one person from another, text features are those aspects of a page of text that differentiate it from others. Text features not only make printed pages unique; they can also significantly affect comprehension. For example,

- A page of printed instructions describing how to assemble a child's bicycle is much easier to comprehend if those instructions are accompanied by detailed diagrams.

- Research articles in scholarly medical journals can be confusing to the average layperson because they contain technical terminology.

- A novel that jumps from one time frame to another and then back again is harder to follow than one written chronologically.

These examples illustrate three types of text features that affect comprehension. Wise teachers consider these when they plan instruction. Specifically, we are referring to

- **Reader aids:** any pictorial, typographical, graphic, and structural representations whose purpose is to convey information;

- **Vocabulary:** terminology the author uses to express ideas and concepts; and

- **Text structure:** the organizational pattern the author employs to express his ideas.

Text features vary from one content area to another. For instance, mathematics texts require students to use subject-specific reading skills, such decoding symbols in an equation. In fact, learning "to communicate mathematically" is one of the five general student goals identified by the National Council of Teachers of Mathematics.

Reading skills students need to employ can vary even within a subject area. For example, many students find that reading authors like Melville, Hawthorne, and Conrad is "slow going" because they aren't accustomed to the sentence structure and vocabulary used.

Miller (1997) notes that science and social studies textbooks selected for a grade level are often above the reading level of many students in that grade. Similarly, an examination of math textbooks reveals that even though the mathematical concepts may be grade-level appropriate, the reading level can be one, two, even three years too advanced for the students for whom the books are written (Braselton and Decker, 1994).

In order to anticipate problems that students may have with unique text features, teachers need to take a figurative step back from their subject area during their planning, and look through text material they plan to assign as if they were students rather than content area experts. Next, they need to determine how to help students learn the reading skills they will need to comprehend their content area assignments.

Reader Aids

Learning to be aware of features like bold print, headings, italics, bulleted material, and pictures can help students become more effective readers. Strategies such as Reciprocal Teaching (p. 128) and Survey, Question, Read, Recite, Review (SQ3R, p. 130) require that students notice and work with text features before reading. Previewing text passages for reader aids can give the reader clues about concepts that are important and require attention. It can also

McREL

provide her with a mental framework to use for organizing ideas as she reads, which aids retention and recall.

Two other types of text features that impact comprehension, vocabulary and text structure, will be examined in detail in the pages that follow.

Text Features: Vocabulary

> "A word is not a crystal, transparent and unchanged; it is the skin of a living thought and may vary greatly in color and content according to the circumstance and time in which it is used."
>
> Oliver Wendell Holmes, Jr.

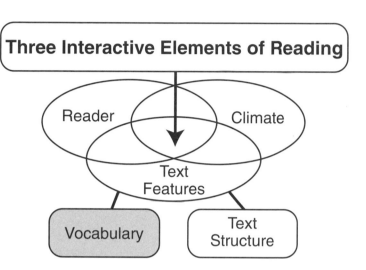

Introduction

Often, the teaching of vocabulary is restricted (or relegated) to the language arts teacher. However, all content areas need to focus on vocabulary instruction. Research conducted in the past ten years reveals that vocabulary knowledge is the single most important factor contributing to reading comprehension. Moreover, studies conducted on the importance of vocabulary instruction demonstrate that it plays a major role in improving comprehension (Laflamme, 1997).

Each content area has its own unique vocabulary or lexicon. In fact, content areas are distinguishable by the terminology and language they use, particularly the labels they use to identify important content area concepts. Content area vocabulary differs greatly from the vocabulary that students study in literature-based classes. Therefore, it is essential that content area teachers incorporate vocabulary work into their planning and instruction.

Armbruster and Nagy (1992) identify three aspects of content area vocabulary that differentiate it from the vocabulary used in literature-based lessons. First, content area vocabulary often consists of **major concepts** that undergird a lesson or unit. Therefore, it is critical that students have a clear understanding of what these concepts mean. A student who cannot explain the meaning of *perspective* after an art lesson on this drawing technique probably has failed to grasp an essential portion of the lesson. In contrast, if a student does not understand a word like *desultory* in a short story, his understanding of the story is not likely to be affected.

A second reason why content area vocabulary terms need to be explicitly taught is that these terms are rarely associated with concepts that students already know. For instance, a student who encounters the term *photosynthesis* for the first time while reading his science text is confronting an entirely new concept. He has no prior knowledge with which he can connect this term. Nothing in his experience can provide him with a synonym to which he can liken it. Learning new vocabulary in literature-based lessons, however, often involves learning a new label for a concept the student already understands. For example, if *indolent* is used to describe a character in a story, the reader can easily understand it when it is compared to familiar synonyms, like *idle* and *lazy*.

A third difference between content area vocabulary and the vocabulary students encounter in reading lessons is that content area terms are often semantically related. Students studying a unit on weather might confront the terms *cirrus, cumulus,* and *stratus.* How thoroughly a student understands the concept of cirrus clouds will affect what she understands cumulus clouds to be. In contrast, vocabulary words in a language arts lesson are often completely unrelated in meaning. Knowing the meaning of *edifice,* for example, will not affect a student's comprehension of other terms in the lesson, such as *despot,* or *cache.*

McREL

Recent research in early childhood literacy suggests that children's early background and knowledge base play a significant role in learning and in vocabulary development. A lack of experience, or limited experiences, can become a barrier to learning new concepts and ideas, especially for children whose exposure to life has come primarily from TV. For this reason, teachers need to be sensitive to the level of experience their students bring to class and to find creative ways to help students expand their knowledge base through direct experience, discussion, analogies, and explanations for content area concepts.

Instructional Implications

Although teachers know that they should do something about vocabulary instruction in their content areas, many are unsure how to tackle this issue. Consequently, some teachers reduce instruction to having students use glossaries and dictionaries to look up and memorize word meanings. Although this method has been used in classrooms for years, it simply is not effective, as it does not transfer into students' everyday language. First, looking up words in a dictionary does not promote real understanding or long-term recall, because it isolates the learning of vocabulary from the exploration of the subject matter. Moreover, because content area vocabulary often represent major concepts in a unit, instruction needs to go beyond simply defining the terms. Students need strategies that can help them learn what new concepts mean and see the connections between these concepts. Rote memorization will not provide students any means of making these connections.

A common practice is preteaching vocabulary at the beginning of a unit of study. There is some disagreement among reading researchers about whether vocabulary terms should be taught prior to students reading text passages or taught during and after they have read them. A number of studies have shown that intensive preteaching of vocabulary can improve comprehension (Laflamme, 1997). Other experts (Armbruster and Nagy, 1992) advocate

McREL

teaching target vocabulary during or after reading: "An important goal of content area lessons is to help students learn how to learn from reading so that they can independently acquire information from text" (p.550). Both viewpoints have merit, and teachers need to experiment with each to find what works best for their students.

Regardless of the timing of vocabulary instruction, students learn content area terms best through first-hand, purposeful interaction with these concepts in their environment. When it isn't possible to provide students with direct experience, teachers can construct opportunities for students to observe their use through more contrived experiences, such as demonstrations, field trips, or audiovisual examples. For students to gain a thorough understanding of technical concepts, teachers need to provide multiple opportunities for students to learn how these words are conceptually related (Vacca and Vacca, 1993).

Of course, teachers cannot teach every unfamiliar word that students might encounter in their text. In addition to teachers selecting which concepts will be the focus of the unit, Haggard (1982) suggests letting students select their own words by previewing the readings. Working in teams, students develop a list of unfamiliar terms that they believe will be crucial for understanding the focus of the unit. Student-selected words are listed on chart paper, and each team is asked to defend its selections. The teacher then modifies this list by deleting terms judged to be less-important and adding any vocabulary concepts that students overlooked; she clearly explains her reasons for including certain words and eliminating others so that students understand how to identify crucial words in content reading.

After vocabulary terms are selected, teachers need to determine which strategies will offer students the best insights into concept meanings and also the relationships among concepts.

McREL

There are many vocabulary development strategies teachers can use. This manual discusses eight on pp. 70-89:

- Concept Definition Mapping

- Frayer Model

- Prereading Predictions

- Semantic Feature Analysis

- Semantic Mapping

- Stephens Vocabulary Elaboration Strategy (SVES)

- Student VOC Strategy

- Word Sorts

In summary, learning vocabulary in the content areas often means learning entirely new concepts. Therefore, content area teachers should offer students a variety of opportunities to work with and experience these concepts in context and to explore the relationships among them.

No matter which vocabulary development strategies teachers elect to use, the key to encouraging students to build their vocabulary is the attitude their teacher displays toward vocabulary learning. When students see that their teacher is enthusiastic about learning new concepts, and models how he derives the meaning of new concepts while reading, they learn that vocabulary development is not only important but is also a lifelong process.

Eight Principles of Vocabulary Instruction

1. Be enthusiastic about content area language and the power it can offer to students who understand how to use these words effectively.

2. Remember that learning involves making connections between what we already know and new information. Relate new vocabulary words to experiences and concepts that students already know.

3. Limit the number of words taught in each unit; concentrate on key concepts.

4. Teach concepts in semantically-related clusters, so that students can see clearly the associations among related concepts.

5. Model how to use graphic organizers.

6. Allow students enough practice in working with strategies and graphic organizers so that their use becomes a habit.

7. Use dictionaries and glossaries appropriately.

8. Repeatedly model how to determine a word's meaning in text materials. Observing the process you use will help students know what to do when they encounter unfamiliar words outside of the classroom.

McREL

Text Features: Text Structure

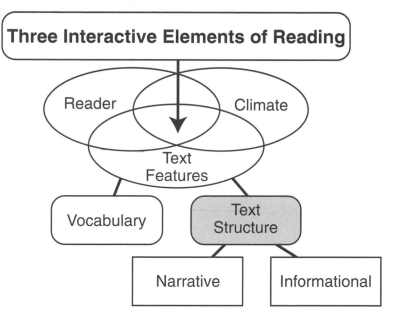

Introduction

Effective readers construct meaning from text by making connections between what they already know and the new information they encounter. Making meaningful connections involves a number of skills: locating and identifying what information is most important; recognizing the relationships that exist among the ideas presented in the text, and between those ideas and what the reader already knows; and organizing all of these ideas into a mental pattern or sequence that makes sense to the reader.

Skilled authors spend considerable time before they write determining what kind of organizational pattern will best convey their ideas. They may decide that developing their ideas clearly requires that they organize them into a comparison/contrast pattern. Or they might decide to employ one of the following patterns: a descriptive pattern, an episode pattern, a process/cause-effect pattern; a time sequence pattern, a concept pattern, or a generalization/principle pattern (Marzano et al., 1997). Familiarity with these patterns in text greatly enhances comprehension and learning. Knowing which pattern is being used helps the reader

- locate information in the text;

- differentiate between what is important and unimportant;

- mentally sequence the main ideas in a logical order;

- synthesize ideas that appear in different locations in the text or from a number of texts;

- link new information to what is already known; and

- restructure and revise prior knowledge to take into account this new information (Jones, Palincsar, Ogle, and Carr, 1987).

Content area teachers can help students improve reading comprehension by making sure they understand

- the difference between narrative text and informational text;

- the organizational patterns typically used in each;

- how to recognize these different organizational patterns; and

- the kinds of questions each pattern is intended to help answer.

Comparing Narrative and Informational Text: an Illustration

In order to experience the similarities and differences between these two kinds of text structures, read the selections indented below. These passages—one narrative, the other informational—address the same topic: electric shock therapy. Read each selection and determine the similarities and differences between them.

Narrative Text

"Man, what they got going in there?" McMurphy asks Harding.

"In there? Why, that's right, isn't it? You haven't had the pleasure. Pity. An experience no human should be without." Harding laces his fingers behind his neck and leans back to look at the door. "That's the Shock Shop I was telling you about some time back, my friend, the EST, Electric-Shock Therapy. Those fortunate souls in there are being given a free trip to the moon. No, on second thought, it isn't completely free. You pay for the service with brain cells instead of money and everyone has simply billions of brain cells on deposit. You won't miss a few."

"I personally guarantee it. Completely painless. One flash and you're unconscious immediately. No gas, no needle, no sledgehammer. Absolutely painless. The thing is, no one ever wants another one. You… change. You forget things. It's as if" — he presses his hands against his temples, shutting his eyes — "It's as if the jolt sets off a wild carnival wheel of images, emotions, memories. These wheels, you've seen them; the barker takes your bet and pushes a button. Clang! With light and sound and numbers round and round and round in a whirlwind, and maybe you win with what you have to play again. Pay the man for another spin, son, pay the man."

One Flew Over the Cuckoo's Nest, Ken Kesey, pp.162, 164.

Informational Text

Holmberg discusses a number of biochemical and hormonal changes that have been reported in conjunction with Electric Shock Therapy. Hyperglycemia of one to several hours duration is a constant phenomenon. There is also an increase in nitrogen compounds, potassium, calcium, phosphorous, and steroids in the blood.

Holmberg also lists certain specific biochemical changes within the brain, and especially in the brain stem, which are increased but there is no change in brain amine oxidase activity. The increase in seratonin is attributed to the electric stimulus and does not appear to be related to the intensity of the convulsion.

Some impairment of memory occurs almost constantly with EST. This impairment may range from a mild tendency to forget names or dates to a severe confusion. The amnesia may be both anterograde and retrograde. It is often disturbing to the patient and may continue for several weeks following the conclusion of treatment. The impairment of memory usually disappears within a month.

Depression—Causes and Treatment, Aaron T. Beck, M.D., pp.306, 307

After comparing these two structural patterns, give some thought to the following reflective questions:

- What are some major similarities between the texts, some major differences?

- What prior knowledge did you find yourself using to help you complete this task?

- As you read each text, describe the thought pattern you use to analyze each text.

- What are some major learnings you will carry forward from this activity?

- How might you use this type of activity with your students?

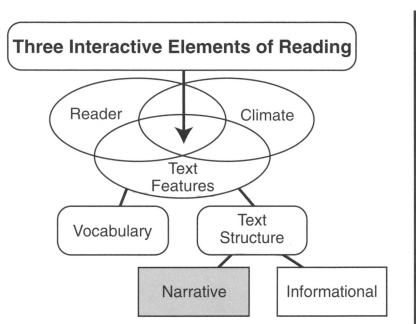

Three Interactive Elements of Reading

Reader · Climate · Text Features · Vocabulary · Text Structure · Narrative · Informational

Narrative Text

Narrative text is writing in which a story is told; the details may be fictional or based on fact. Typically, the events described in narrative text are written sequentially. History texts may read as narratives, but history texts are written to inform. The primary purpose of narrative writing is to entertain. Novels depict numerous episodes of action. Short stories may only contain a few or even one episode. Nevertheless, both relate a causal chain of events: each event in the story leads to another, as the protagonist, or main character, tries to reach a goal or solve a problem.

Elements that are basic to narrative text include a setting, characters, plot, conflict, and theme. Some literary authorities label these elements "story grammar." That is, just as sentence grammar is used to explain and specify how sentences are constructed, story grammar delineates the basic parts of a story and how those work together to create a well-constructed tale (Vacca and Vacca, 1993).

Science fiction:
a fictional story that usually considers the question "What if...?" about some current or projected scientific and technological developments. (Examples: *Fahrenheit 451*; *A Wrinkle in Time*)

Fantasy:
a story in which the characters, setting, or events are completely imaginary and would never be found in real life. (Examples: *The Hobbit*; *The Lion, the Witch, and the Wardrobe*; *Faust*)

Fable:
A short tale that teaches a lesson, often using animals as characters. (Examples: *Animal Farm*; *Aesop's Fables*)

Folk tale:
A story of unknown origin, but well known in a particular culture through repeated telling. (Examples: "Strega Nona"; "John Henry"; "Why the Sun and Moon Live in the Sky")

Myth:
A story passed down through oral tradition that explains natural phenomena, religion, or history of a race (Examples: "Odysseus and the Cyclops"; "The Legend of King Arthur and the Knights of the Round Table"; *The Iliad*)

Following is an example of story grammar found in *The Rainmaker* by John Grisham:

1. **Setting:** Memphis, its legal community, and its court system.

2. **Characters:** Rudy Baylor is the main character. He meets his first legal clients: Miss Birdie, a volunteer at the Cypress Gardens Senior Citizen Building, and Donny Ray Black, a young man who needs a bone-marrow transplant. Dot and Buddy Black are the parents of Donny Ray.

3. **Problem or conflict:** Rudy Baylor discovers that a very large insurance company is not only denying benefits to his client, Donny Ray Black, but has a history of denying benefits to subscribers.

> "'Begin at the beginning,' the king said gravely, 'and go till you come to the end; then stop.'"
>
> Lewis Carroll,
> *Alice's Adventures in Wonderland,*
> (1865), p.12.

4. **Plot:** The judge initially presiding over the case suddenly dies, and the newly appointed judge detests the fraudulent practices of insurance companies. Rudy goes to the company to take depositions of different employees only to discover that several have been released from their position or resigned. The law firm representing the insurance company taps Rudy's phone, and when he discovers his phone is illegally tapped, he plays games with the law firm by planting false information.

5. **Resolution:** The case goes to court and is decided in favor of the plaintiffs. They are awarded fifty million dollars. The insurance company files for protection under the bankruptcy code and therefore is not liable for the fifty million dollars. It is, however, a moral and ethical victory.

Determining the theme of a story requires inferential thinking. The reader reflects on the story's relevant details in light of his own experience and draws some conclusion about the author's message, the moral of the story, and what the story "says" to him. A student's ability to identify the theme will vary, depending on his level of background knowledge, the experiences he has had in life, and his ability to engage in inferential thinking.

Teachers can help students learn how to identify story grammar by generating questions that ask students to examine:

- what event occurs at the beginning of the story that sets things in motion.

- what the protagonist's reaction is to that event.

- what problem the protagonist faces or what goal he sets for himself.

- what he does to accomplish that goal or solve that problem.

- what other events his actions precipitate.

- what the characters say about the events, about themselves, and about one another.

- what the high point or climax of the story seems to be.

- how the protagonist does or does not resolve the problem or reach his goal.

- when and where the events occur, and how this affects what happens.

- what the protagonist(s) learn about himself (themselves) or about life in general.

- what the author's message seems to be.

Asking these kinds of questions and consistently discussing the events of the story in chronological order will strengthen students' understanding of story grammar in general, as well as show them how to identify and analyze story grammar when reading independently. (See Figure 3.)

Strategies learners can use to understand narrative text (on pp. 90-103) include:

- Character Map
- Directed Reading/Thinking Activity (DR/TA)
- Probable Passages
- Story Frame
- Story Grammar/Maps

McREL

- Story Mapping through Circular Pictures

- Venn Diagram

Setting
- When and where does the story take place?
- Why do you think the author chose this setting?

Characters
- List the main characters in the story.
- Who is the most important? Why?
- Describe what he/she is like. For each character trait, explain what he/she does, says, and what others say about him/her that reveals that trait.
- Is the main character believable? How do you feel about him/her?

Problem/Goal/Conflict
- What is the main character's problem or goal?
- Why is this a problem/goal for the main character?
- What does this tell us about the main character?
- How do other characters or things contribute to this problem/goal?
- Would this be a problem for you? Why or why not?

Plot
- Explain what happens in the story.
- Is what happens believable?
- What is the high point or climax of the story?
- How is the main character's problem solved or goal achieved?
- Does the main character change or learn anything as a result of what happens? Explain.
- If you were the main character, how would you have reacted?

Theme
- What is the author's message/moral/theme? How do you know?
- How can you apply this message to your own life?

<u>Figure 3.</u> **Sample questions**

Notes

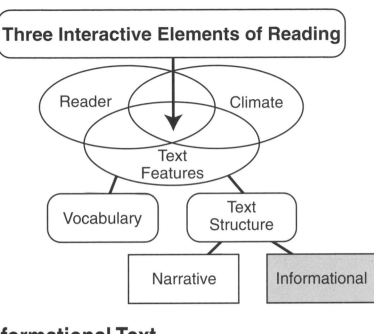

Three Interactive Elements of Reading

Reader   Climate

Text Features

Vocabulary   Text Structure

Narrative   Informational

Informational Text

Typically, informational text is written to inform or persuade. Some teachers call informational text *expository* text. Examples of informational text are textbook chapters, newspaper and magazine articles, and reference material. The ideas contained in informational text can be organized in a number of different ways. Following are seven common organizational patterns adapted from the work of Marzano et al. (1997) and Jones, Palincsar, Ogle, and Carr (1987):

- Chronological sequence: organizes events in a time sequence.

- Comparison and contrast: organizes information about two or more topics according to their similarities and differences.

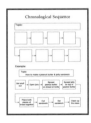

- Concept/definition: organizes information about a word or phrase that represents a **generalized** idea of a class of persons, places, things, and events (e.g., dictatorship, economics, culture, mass production). Concept/definition text defines a

concept by presenting its characteristics or attributes, and sometimes examples of each.

- Description: organizes facts that describe the characteristics of **specific** persons, places, things, and events. These characteristics do not need to be given in any particular order.

- Episode: organizes a large body of information about specific events. This information includes the time and place, specific people, specific duration, specific sequence of incidents that occur, and the event's particular cause and effect. An example of an episode pattern might be found in an account of Watergate: when it occurred, who was involved, how long it lasted, the sequence of events, what caused it and what the effects were.

- Generalization/principle: organizes information into general statements with supporting examples.

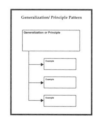

- Process/cause-effect: organizes information into a series of steps leading to a specific product; or organizes information in a causal sequence that leads to a specific outcome.

When readers are familiar with the text's organizational pattern, they are able to read the information with specific questions in mind. That is, each organizational pattern suggests a series of questions that will be answered within the text. Answering these questions helps the reader comprehend the author's message. Figure 4 lists some of the questions implied by each pattern.

Skilled authors incorporate certain signal words, linking expressions, or transitions that connect one idea to another. When

Chronological Sequence
- What sequence of events is being described?
- What are the major incidents that occur?
- How is this pattern revealed in the text?

Comparison and Contrast
- What items are being compared?
- What is it about them that are being compared? What characteristics of the items form the basis of the comparison?
- What characteristics do they have in common; how are these items alike?
- In what way are these items different?
- What conclusion does the author reach about the degree of similarity or difference between the items?
- How did the author reveal this pattern?

Concept/definition
- What concept is being defined?
- What are its attributes or characteristics?
- How does it work, or what does it do?
- What examples are given for each of the attributes or characteristics?
- How is this pattern revealed in the text?

Description
- What specific person, place, thing, or event is being described?
- What are its most important attributes or characteristics?
- Would the description change if the order of the attributes were changed?
- Why is this description important?

Episode
- What event is being explained or described?
- What is the setting where the event occurs?
- Who are the major figures or characters that play a part in this event?
- What are the specific incidents or events that occur? In what order do they happen?
- What caused this event?
- What effects has this event had on the people involved?
- What effects has this event had on society in general?

Generalization/principle
- What generalization is the author making or what principle is being explained?
- What facts, examples, statistics, and expert opinion are given that support the generalization or that explain the principle?
- Do these details appear in a logical order?
- Are enough facts, examples, statistics, and expert opinion included to clearly support or explain the generalization/principle?

Process/cause-effect
- What process or subject is being explained?
- What are the specific steps in the process, or what specific causal events occur?
- What is the product or end result of the process; or what is the outcome of the causal events?

Figure 4. Questions suggested by organizational patterns

teachers model for students how to recognize different text patterns, they can point out these signal words and transitions as clues to the organizational pattern. (See Figure 5.)

Expert readers not only recognize these patterns in text; they also use these patterns to impose meaning on text. In other words, a reader could recognize that text is written in a descriptive pattern, and yet select a comparison-contrast frame of mind to compare the description he is reading to something else he knows about already. Another advantage of text structure knowledge is that when textbooks are not well-organized (and some of them are not), skilled readers are able to impose a structure of their own to organize the information into something that makes sense to them. Thus, organizational patterns can exist both on paper and in the mind of the reader (Jones, Palincsar, Ogle, and Carr; 1987).

Notes

Chronological Sequence	Concept/Definition	Episode	Process/Cause-Effect
after	for instance	a few days/months later	accordingly
afterward	in other words	around this time	as a result of
as soon as	is characterized by	as it is often called	because
before	put another way	as a result of	begins with
during	refers to	because of	consequently
finally	that is	began when	effects of
first	thus	consequently	finally
following	usually	first	first
immediately	**Description**	for this reason	for this reason
initially	above	lasted for	how to
later	across	led to	how
meanwhile	along	shortly thereafter	if...then
next	appears to be	since then	in order to
not long after	as in	subsequently	is caused by
now	behind	this led to	leads/led to
on (date)	below	when	may be due to
preceding	beside		next
second	between	**Generalization/Principle**	so that
soon	down	additionally	steps involved
then	in back of	always	therefore
third	in front of	because of	thus
today	looks like	clearly	when...then
until	near	conclusively	
when	on top of	first	
Comparison/Contrast	onto	for instance	
although	outside	for example	
as well as	over	furthermore	
as opposed to	such as	generally	
both	to the right/left	however	
but	under	if...then	
compared with		in fact	
different from		it could be argued that	
either...or		moreover	
even though		most convincing	
however		never	
instead of		not only...but also	
in common		often	
on the other hand		second	
otherwise		therefore	
similar to		third	
similarly		truly	
still		typically	
yet			

<u>Figure 5.</u> Signal words for determining text patterns

Instructional Implications

Teach students about organizational patterns, one at a time, through a series of mini-lessons. Suggested steps in this instructional strategy are:

1. Activate students' prior knowledge of text structure and organization of information. This can be done through brainstorming, or by posing a problem for students to solve, such as how they would order their ideas if they wanted to explain to a child how to dribble a basketball, or convince their

Notes

parents to give them a raise in their allowance, etc. Discuss why they chose to organize their ideas in that order.

2. Introduce an organizational pattern. Explain what the pattern is, its characteristics, when/why writers use it, signal words of note, and what questions this pattern typically answers.

3. Provide an example of this pattern in the textbook or in a trade book. Informational trade books offer in-depth information on a variety of content area topics and often organize information more logically and coherently than content area textbooks (Moss, 1991). Model for students how to tell the example fits into this category of organizational patterns.

4. Provide students with a graphic organizer that they can use to map out the information contained in the sample. Demonstrate how to fill in the organizer. Explain that having a visual representation of how a text is organized will aid comprehension and retention.

5. Ask students to locate another example of this pattern in their textbook, newspapers, magazines, or trade books. Students can then use a graphic organizer to diagram the information in the example they select.

6. Have students write paragraphs using the pattern. This last step reinforces understanding and enhances learning: Research indicates that readers who are taught to write and edit different types of informational text improve their reading comprehension of content textbooks (Raphael, Kirschner, and Englert, 1988). Students select a topic, gather any information they need, and map that information onto a graphic organizer. Using this as a visual map, they write a rough draft and add signal words where appropriate. Students can edit one another's paragraphs. With this input, students revise their rough draft, edit it, and write a final copy.

Primary Grades and Reading in the Content Areas

Typically, children learn to read using basal readers. They have multiple opportunities to interact with and learn narrative text structure. Eventually, students are handed informational text. At that point they are expected to make the leap from *learning to read* through stories written in familiar chronological order to *learning to read to obtain information* from content area text that is organized in entirely different ways (Anthony and Raphael, 1989; cf. Barton, 1997). Although informational text is being introduced at earlier points in the primary grades, instruction in working with informational text in many cases still needs to be more focused and intensive.

In a survey conducted by Olson and Gee (1991), 85 percent of primary teachers (first through third grades) acknowledged the value of six teaching practices in particular: previewing concepts and vocabulary, using concrete manipulatives to develop concepts, requiring retellings, developing summaries, visualizing information, and brainstorming. Teachers in the survey identified five strategies as being effective in helping their students read content area passages:

1. Group Summarizing (p. 112)
2. Informational Paragraph Frames (p. 114)
3. K-W-L (p. 116)
4. Semantic Mapping (p. 134)
5. Sensory Imagery (p. 136)

Strategies to help all learners acquire an understanding of how to read for information (pp. 104-141) are as follows:

- Anticipation Guides
- Directed Reading/Thinking Activity (DR/TA)
- Graphic Organizers
- Group Summarizing
- Informational Paragraph Frames
- K-W-L (What I Know, What I Want to Learn, What I Learned)
- Pairs Read
- Prereading Plan (PreP)

- Problematic Situations
- Proposition/Support Outline
- Reciprocal Teaching
- SQ 3R (Survey, Question, Read, Recite, Review)
- Search Strategy
- Semantic Mapping
- Sensory Imagery
- Structured Note-taking
- "Think-alouds"

Conclusion

Our desired outcome for student reading is the construction of meaning. The text structures, organizational patterns, and strategies introduced in this section serve as a resource for readers needing a framework to organize text; however, an awareness of organizational patterns is meant to be a tool to support comprehension, not an end in itself.

Strategic Processing

Section 2

Strategic Processing

> "Be the change you wish to see."
>
> **Gandhi**

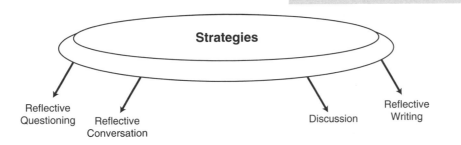

Metacomprehension

Think about a particular activity you engaged in recently—teaching a specific class, playing a game of tennis or golf, working out, preparing a meal, even playing a video game. Create a mental movie of what you did, what you thought, and how you behaved as you engaged in this activity. As you probably wanted to accomplish the task with some degree of success, you may remember thinking about what you were doing and evaluating how successful your actions were. Just as you are doing now, you may have stepped outside yourself to observe or monitor the effectiveness of your actions and attitude at different points during the activity. If necessary, you adjusted your behavior so you would be more likely to achieve your goal. You were strategic and reflective as you performed this activity.

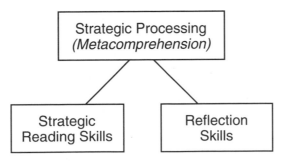

When a learner is strategic and reflective about her thinking and learning, cognitive psychologists would say she is utilizing metacognition skills. Metacognition is thinking about one's thinking. Various reading researchers (Gavelek and Raphael, 1985; Osman and Hannafin, 1992; Caverly, Mandeville, and Nicholson, 1995) have used the term *metacomprehension* to refer to being strategic and reflective about reading comprehension.

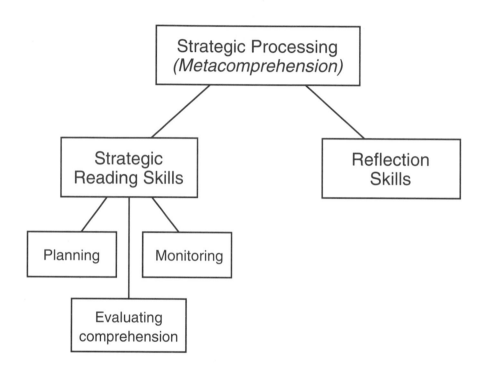

Effective readers are **strategic** in the way they attack text material. (1) They consciously *plan* for their reading:

- They preview the material to get a sense of its contents, scope, and organization.

- From this preview, they activate prior knowledge about the topic and formulate some predictions and questions about what will be covered.

- They consider what kinds of reading skills they will need to use, based on their preview and on their knowledge of what the particular subject or content area typically requires.

- They clarify their purpose for reading, and select a reading style that will help them achieve that goal.

(2) As they read, they *monitor* their reading process:

- On one level, they are engaged with the content material of the text, making mental notes about important concepts, revising predictions, answering questions, and noting main and subordinate ideas.

- On another level, they are observing and assessing their attitude toward the task and their reading style, and whether these are helping accomplish the purpose.

- They adjust their attitude and style as needed to improve comprehension—perhaps slowing their pace, restraining any impulsive desire to stop reading, redirecting their focus, or selecting fix-up strategies (e.g., rereading confusing passages and examining the context of unfamiliar words to ascertain meaning).

(3) After they read, they *evaluate* how well they understood the text:

- They summarize the text's main ideas. If needed, they reread or review certain passages.

- They appraise their learning in terms of their original purpose, and strategize how they might demonstrate that understanding if asked to do so.

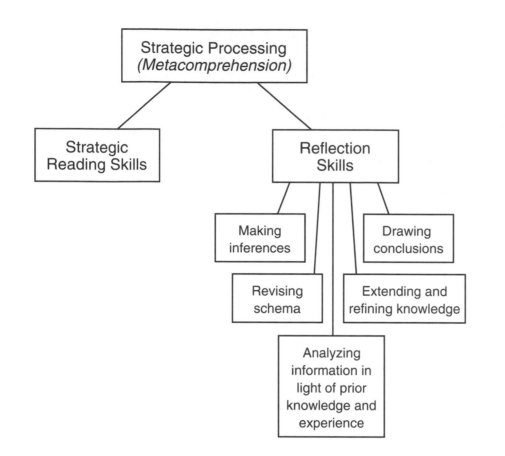

In addition to being strategic about their reading process, ideal readers are **reflective.**

- They mull over the text ideas both as they read and after they finish reading, weighing the information in light of their reading purpose.

- They analyze how the material aligns with their prior knowledge and experience, measuring it against what they believe, what they know, and what they have experienced.

- They make inferences and draw conclusions about what they read.

- They revise their schema as needed, incorporating new learning into their knowledge base.

- After reading, they continually extend and refine what they have learned, deepening their understanding of the material.

Few teachers would argue the importance of students acquiring metacognition and metacomprehension skills. Exactly how critical these skills are, especially in students who struggle with school work, is documented in a rather startling 1993 commentary in *Education Week*. Stanley Pogrow, assistant professor at the University of Arizona and developer of the Higher Order Thinking Skills program, wrote that most students over third grade who have learning difficulties serious enough for placement in special programs do not have problems with basic reading skills; rather, these students lack metacomprehension skills, and therefore are unable to systematically construct meaning or utilize strategies efficiently (Pogrow, 1993; Caverly, Mandeville, and Nicholson, 1995). Clearly, we need to train students in how to be strategic readers who are able to plan for, monitor, and evaluate their reading process, and who reflect on the meaning of what they read in terms of their prior knowledge and experience.

In Section 1, we examined ways to help students *plan* for reading by (1) activating their prior knowledge, (2) previewing the passage for text features and unfamiliar vocabulary, (3) making predictions, (4) setting purpose, and (5) practicing productive habits of mind.

Monitoring the effectiveness of one's reading behaviors on comprehension means (1) being able to observe and assess those behaviors, and (2) being able to select alternative behaviors and strategies as needed to improve comprehension.

Acquiring these metacognitive skills requires instruction and practice. Ineffective readers often are not aware of their thinking or their level of comprehension as they read. Teachers can use "think-alouds" (Davey, 1983) to demonstrate metacognitive processing. With think-alouds, the teacher makes her own thinking explicit by verbalizing her thoughts while reading orally. Students observe how the teacher creates mental pictures, deals with unfamiliar vocabulary, revises predictions, and so on. Novice readers are often surprised to learn what goes on in a practiced reader's mind while she reads. "Think-alouds" illustrate how students should interact with the text.

Asking students process questions can also alert them to the kind of thinking and comprehending that should be happening as they read. Questions to Promote Metacomprehension (Figure 6) can be used to help students plan for and monitor their comprehension and *evaluate* the effectiveness of the reading skills and strategies they use.

Pre-reading Questions	**Questions to Ask While Reading**	**Post-reading Questions**
• Preview the passage. What do you think it will be about?	• What do you think the main ideas of the passage are so far?	• What were the main ideas in this passage? Were your predictions accurate?
• What are some things you already know about the topic?	• What kind of graphic organizer would you use to begin organizing these ideas?	• What other information do you want to remember from this passage? How will you help yourself remember this information?
• What are your reading goals? What do you hope to learn from reading this passage?	• What did you picture in your mind about these ideas while you were reading?	• Did you accomplish your reading goal?
• What is your purpose for reading? What will you be required to do with the information you learn from reading? (Take a quiz or multiple choice test? Complete a performance activity? Write an evaluative essay?) How will this affect the way you will read the passage?	• Is the information in this passage similar to anything you have learned before? How?	• Which reading and learning strategies did you find most helpful, and why?
	• What are you wondering about at this point in your reading? Write down a question.	• What parts of the passage interested you the most? What ideas made you think?
• What strategies could you use as you read the passage to help you understand what you are reading?	• What is your attitude toward reading the passage at this point? Do you need to modify any of your behaviors, attitudes, or resources in order to reach your goal?	• How has your thinking changed as a result of reading this passage?
• How will you know you understood the message intended by the author?		

Figure 6. Questions to promote metacomprehension

As John Dewey noted, "we learn by doing if we reflect on what we have done." Certainly, ideal readers reflect on the content while they are reading, measuring it in light of what they know and believe. Guided, active reading requires that teachers pose questions at strategic points in the passage, questions that demand a certain amount of introspection and reflection while students are reading the material.

Effective readers also reflect on what they have read once they close their texts. Reflection deepens understanding. In the next few pages, we offer suggestions on how to encourage reflective thought through questioning, writing-to-learn activities, discussion, and conversation.

Reflective Questioning

Because questioning helps readers think about what they read, it is helpful to have a framework for developing and asking questions. QAR, or Question/Answer Relationships (Raphael, 1984, 1986), is a strategy that is not only an effective framework or taxonomy for developing questions, but also a tool that transfers the control of the questioning process from teacher to students.

Students are taught four types of questions: "right there," "think and search," "the author and you," and "on your own." (See p. 145.) When students are able to recognize each type of question and understand that each demands an answer found in a particular place—either in text or in their experience—they are better able to answer questions correctly. They are also able to generate similar questions on their own to clarify and enhance their understanding of the material. When QAR is taught to students and practiced in class for as little as eight weeks, reading comprehension improves significantly, with average and below-average students showing the greatest improvement (Miller, 1997; Richardson and Morgan, 1994).

Other instructional strategies that emphasize reflective questioning are Concept Question Chain (p. 142.), and Reciprocal Teaching (p. 128).

Reflective Writing

The questions students ask when given a writing assignment are very revealing: "Does this count?"; "How long does it have to be?"; "Does spelling/neatness count?" Somehow students have gotten the idea that writing is simply another "hoop" they have to jump through to satisfy the teacher. To many students, writing means the finished product, to be written for and graded by the teacher, who alone knows the criteria. Perhaps students view the process of writing in this light because teachers traditionally have used writing only as a product: the essay test, theme, or lab report to be completed at the end of the lesson or unit.

However, the act of writing involves thinking; it requires active engagement with content. As students write, they construct meaning around the subject matter. They make connections between the topic and themselves. They discover what they know and what they do not know. Writing is a tool for learning. In fact, writing is fundamental to thinking about and acquiring knowledge in all content areas as well as to communicating that knowledge (Fulwiler, 1987).

Writing-to-learn activities differ from essays, reports and themes in that they are short, exploratory, and often written for an audience other than the teacher. In fact, although grammar and mechanics always "count," the purpose of writing-to-learn activities is to **reflect** on what one has learned, to develop some parameters around it, and to make meaningful, personal connections between it and the writer's life experience. Therefore, assessing writing-to-learn assignments means evaluating a student's writing in light of who he is and the depth of thought he displays.

Some teachers are reluctant to incorporate writing-to-learn activities because of the additional paper load it might create. However, there are numerous creative ways that teachers use to "keep it simple," for instance:

- They do not grade every single assignment.
- They simply monitor with a check whether the student attempted a response or not.
- They check off items on a checklist of criteria they have previously shared with students.
- They use feedback forms with stems of statements they can quickly fill in, like "I like what you said about..."; or "When I read what you wrote, it reminded me of..."; "Have you thought about...?"; or "I'd like to read more about your personal

experience with...."

- They have students read and comment on one another's writing.

Guidelines for developing writing-to-learn topics are:

- They should be short (i.e., students are given "think time," but write for only five minutes).

- They should require creative thinking and exploration of the text material (e.g., integration—what this means to *me.*)

- If possible, the intended audience should be someone other than the teacher. Students may write more carefully if they think someone other than the teacher will be reading it. Consider putting all student responses on the bulletin board, not just the superior papers.

- The kinds of assignments and formats should vary (e.g., learning log entry; analogy; poem; editorial; letter to the textbook publisher or a friend).

For examples of reflective writing activities, see pp. 142-164.

Discussion

Discussion helps students to clarify their understanding of text, refine their thinking, share their ideas, and explore related issues. In the past, discussion often was a prompting session: the teacher posed a series of teacher-generated questions on what students should have read. Questions stayed on the literal level, and students regurgitated facts from the text.

Thankfully, discussion is viewed now as a learning tool that stimulates thinking and that helps students to extend and refine their understanding of the content they read. Two forms of discussion, each with a different amount of structure, can help students interact with the content and with one another.

Guided Discussion

When your teaching goal is informational in nature—that is, you want to use discussion to help students clarify their understanding of content they have read—guided discussion techniques are appropriate. In guided discussion, the teacher uses questions or teacher-developed study guide materials to direct student thinking. In addition to designing and posing questions, the teacher's role is to encourage student questions about the content and to provide additional information and clarification when needed (Vacca and Vacca, 1993).

While guided discussion is useful if the teacher encourages students to be active participants, it can degenerate into more of a lecture, with the teacher both asking and answering his questions. In this case, students quickly learn that the teacher doesn't really want to hear their thoughts; they stop participating and simply wait for the teacher to do all of the work.

Another common pitfall in guided discussion is the tendency for teachers to allow a few bright, verbal students to monopolize the discussion. When this happens, the other students feel self-conscious about participating, so they withdraw and do not share their thoughts.

In order to avoid these problems, teachers need to pose questions that require students to interpret the text, to explore what the text means to them, and to share these interpretations with one another. Brophy (1992) maintains that the construction of meaning requires that students interact with one another. Discussion allows students the chance to think through and paraphrase the content, and then "make it their own" by exploring its relationships to their prior knowledge. Teachers can ensure more active participation if they clearly explain the purpose of the discussion, give explicit directions, and model for students the discussion skills of active listening, paraphrasing, and clarifying.

Reflective Discussion

When students have a good grasp of the concepts they are studying, teachers may want to have students engage in a reflective discussion. The purpose of a reflective discussion is to help students extend and refine their knowledge through making judgments, defending their opinions, and through critical and creative thinking. To some teachers, this may feel like more of a risk, because the teacher's role in a reflective discussion shifts from being the leader/authority to being a participant. Teachers willing to assume this risk can guide students into being more independent learners by modeling productive ways of responding and reacting to others' viewpoints and sensitive issues, and by demonstrating how to think critically about difficult concepts discussed in the text (Alvermann, et al., 1988).

A few general guidelines for creating a classroom environment conducive to discussion are:

1. Arrange the desks so students can see each other or break out into smaller discussion groups.

2. Teach, model, and encourage active listening.

3. Clearly articulate the topic under discussion and the goal of the discussion.

4. Ensure that students stick to the topic of the discussion and don't "go off on tangents."

5. Draw out students who are naturally quiet, shy, or reluctant to participate.

6. Avoid any "teacher" behavior that might stifle the discussion (e.g., facial expressions or posture that betrays a judgment about students' opinions).

Three strategies (on pp. 158-164) that can be used to promote effective discussions are:

- Creative Debate
- Discussion Web
- Scored Discussion

Reflective Conversation

Reflective conversation is when a valued peer helps one become aware of his thinking so that he can change his thought processes, thus improving his overt reading behaviors. When a learner not only understands his inner thought processes, but then uses his understanding to improve his reading comprehension, he is on his way to becoming an ideal reader.

Learning is the overall goal of a reflective conversation for both the reader and the coach facilitating the discussion. Reflective coaches encourage and support readers as they move beyond their present abilities into new behaviors and skills. Interestingly, the coach need not be a more expert reader than the person being coached. Technical expertise frequently is less relevant than the ability to enable or empower students to move beyond their current performance (Costa and Garmston, 1994).

A reflective conversation is a nonjudgmental process that can occur before reading, while reading, and after reading. The process highlights the three phases of cognitive processing:

1. The preactive phase
2. The interactive phase
3. The reflective phase

During the preactive phase, the coach asks the reader questions designed to promote thinking and create focus **before reading** the passage. Planning questions might include the following:

- What are some of the things you already know about the passage?
- What are some predictions about the passage?
- What concepts are you trying to understand by reading this passage?
- What are your reading goals? What do you hope to learn or experience by reading this passage?

McREL

- What strategies might you use as you read the passage to help you understand?

- If you encounter difficulty in understanding the passage while reading, in what ways might you overcome the difficulty?

- How will you know you understood the message intended by the author?

During the interactive phase, students read the passage and are invited to reflect on their progress, their thought processes, and their perceptions of their own behavior with the coach. Asking readers to indicate where they are in their reading, to describe their thinking up to that point, and/or to define alternative reading strategies they intend to pursue helps them become aware of their own behaviors and to monitor and adjust as necessary. Questions the coach asks **while reading** are:

- What are you predicting the main idea of the passage to be at this time?

- Explain how you arrived at that conclusion.

- What were the steps of thinking you used?

- Explain the reading strategies most helpful up to this point of reading.

- Label your thinking steps to this point.

- How is the thinking you are using now like _____?

An **after-reading** conference—the reflective phase of cognitive processing—allows the reader to evaluate how well he read and understood the passage, how productive the strategies were, and whether alternative, more efficient strategies could be used in the future. The conference helps the reader analyze his learning and whether he needs to do further reading in order to understand better the concept within the passage. The coach also asks questions of the reader that cause him to think how he will use the information in future learning situations. After-reading questions are as follows:

- How are you feeling about what you read?

- What was the main idea within the passage?

- What reading strategies did you find most helpful, and why?

- How did the main idea compare to your before-reading prediction?

- How do you see yourself using this information in future situations?

- As a result of this reading, what did you learn about yourself that will help you in future reading situations?

- How is this reflective-conversation process working for you? What can I do as the coach to better meet your learning needs?

Reflective conversation involves strategic use of nonjudgmental verbal behaviors such as **silence, accepting, and clarifying.**

When a coach asks the student a reflective question such as, "What are you predicting the passage will be about?", he should then wait silently until she is ready to respond. All too often, the coach only waits one or two seconds after asking the question before asking another one or giving the answer. A coach who waits communicates respect for the learner's reflection and processing time. Waiting for answers also models desirable behaviors of thoughtfulness, reflection, and restraint of impulsivity. When the coach provides the necessary time for thought, the thinking and creativity of the reader's response increases (Rowe, 1974).

Nonjudgmental **acceptance** of responses indicate to the reader that the coach understands what she said—for example, "You're saying the passage is about...." The coach paraphrases by repeating, rephrasing, translating, or summarizing what the reader said. Maintaining the intent and accurate meaning of what the student said is important. The paraphrase is possibly the most powerful of all the nonjudgmental verbal behaviors because it communicates that "I'm attempting to understand you" and that, in turn, says "I value you" (Costa and Garmston, 1994).

Clarifying indicates that the coach does not understand what the learner is saying and more information is required. For example, "Please expand on what you mean by *gas-permeable*. I'm not sure I understand." Clarifying should not be an attempt by the teacher to redirect what the reader is thinking or feeling, nor a subtle way of expressing criticism.

The intent of asking clarifying questions is to help the coach better understand the learner's ideas, feelings, and thought processes. Clarifying contributes to trust because it communicates to the learner that her ideas are worthy of exploration and consideration (Costa and Garmston, 1994).

The intent of reflective conversation is to assist the learner in becoming an ideal reader. The process of reflective conversation is not a common one in our schools. For students to be successful, they must be taught how to conduct reflective conversations as well as how to continually practice nonjudgmental verbal behaviors.

Once students learn how to "listen to hear," to paraphrase what's been said, and to ask nonjudgmental questions, they can effectively conduct a reflective conversation. It is then that they will have learned how to learn.

McREL

Strategic Teaching

SECTION 3

Strategic Teaching

> "Teaching is a constant stream of professional decisions made before, during and after interaction with the students: decisions which, when implemented, increase the probability of learning."
>
> Madeline Hunter, Author of *Mastery Teaching*

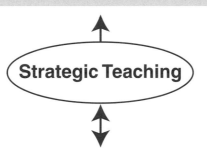

It is estimated that once a student leaves high school, 90 percent of his reading will be to acquire information; only 10 percent will be for pleasure (Daggett, 1990). Planning instruction so that students obtain the skills they will need throughout life is essential. Improvements in higher-level reading skills cannot come about simply by an emphasis on reading instruction in isolation from the other work students do in school. Students must learn to read in all content areas. Every teacher must be a reading teacher.

Teaching strategically means being purposeful and thoughtful about planning instruction. It means analyzing how every aspect of the lesson will contribute to the instructional goal or objective. It means selecting teaching and learning strategies that will enhance student learning. It means helping students acquire the skills they need in order to be self-directed, independent learners.

Specifically, teachers need to help students learn how to:

1. prepare for learning through prereading activities;

2. ensure comprehension through the use of metacognitive strategies during reading; and

3. extend and refine the new knowledge they acquire.

Studies reveal that teachers devote most of their time to presenting new content, but this does little to prepare students to read text assignments or to internalize what they read (Wood and Muth, 1991).

Richardson and Morgan (1994) have developed a framework for strategic teaching that they call PAR, an acronym that stands for

- **P**reparation and Planning before reading: arousing students' curiosity and need to know.

- **A**ssistance and Associations while reading: helping students make connections and monitor their understanding while reading.

- **R**eflection and Readiness for Application after reading: thinking, talking, and writing about key concepts and learning.

Teachers should incorporate learning activities at each stage of PAR, explaining to students why these activities are essential for reading comprehension. Thus, during the Preparation and Planning phase, teachers should offer a variety of techniques to activate and assess prior knowledge and to build background as needed.

Helpful prereading strategies included in this manual are:

- Anticipation Guides
- Problematic Situations
- K-W-L
- DR/TA
- PreP
- Vocabulary strategies

One cannot underestimate the importance of planning prereading activities to increase student readiness to learn. Doug Buehl (1995) uses an apt term for this method of prereading instruction: "frontloading." He asserts that by practicing frontloading techniques (e.g., building background knowledge of the topic, preteaching critical vocabulary concepts, setting a purpose for reading, focusing students' attention on the topic, and cueing students about reading strategies that may be helpful), we not only help increase readiness to learn but also foster strategic reading behavior.

Activities in this manual that teachers can use during what Richardson and Morgan label the Assistance phase include:

- Pairs Read
- Reciprocal Teaching
- Graphic Organizers for mapping ideas and relationships
- SQ3R
- Structured Note-taking
- Sensory Imagery

Activities that address Richardson and Morgan's Reflection phase of the learning process are:

- Informational Paragraph Frames
- Proposition/Support Outlines
- QAR
- RAFT
- Writing-to-Learn
- Learning Logs
- Creative Debate
- Group Summarizing
- Discussion Web
- Scored Discussion.

The checklist on the following page (Figure 7) can assist teachers in strategic planning.

	YES	NO
Have I identified my objectives for this lesson– what I want students to know and be able to do?	❑	❑
Have I previewed the text and determined key concepts/vocabulary students need to know?	❑	❑
Have I included activities and strategies that will help students develop a clear understanding of these key concepts?	❑	❑
Have I selected activities to assess, activate, and build students' background knowledge?	❑	❑
Have I identified the text's organizational pattern(s) and whether it highlights information I consider most important?	❑	❑
If the organizational pattern does not highlight key information, have I determined the frame of mind or pattern I will tell students to use while reading?	❑	❑
Have I selected a suitable graphic organizer students can use to organize key concepts?	❑	❑
Have I decided the purposes students should keep in mind while reading (e.g., whether they will be using the information in a discussion, performance activity, on a quiz)?	❑	❑
Have I developed "during reading" questions that will prompt students to employ metacognitive skills?	❑	❑
Have I selected post-reading questions and activities that require students to make meaningful connections, and to deepen their understanding by applying what they have learned?	❑	❑

Figure 7: Teacher's self-evaluation checklist

In summary, strategic teaching involves careful planning for learning before, during, and after text reading. We maintain that by sharing a variety of strategies with students, by explaining their value, and by repeatedly modeling and having students practice these behaviors, teachers will help students learn how to become self-directed, independent learners.

McREL

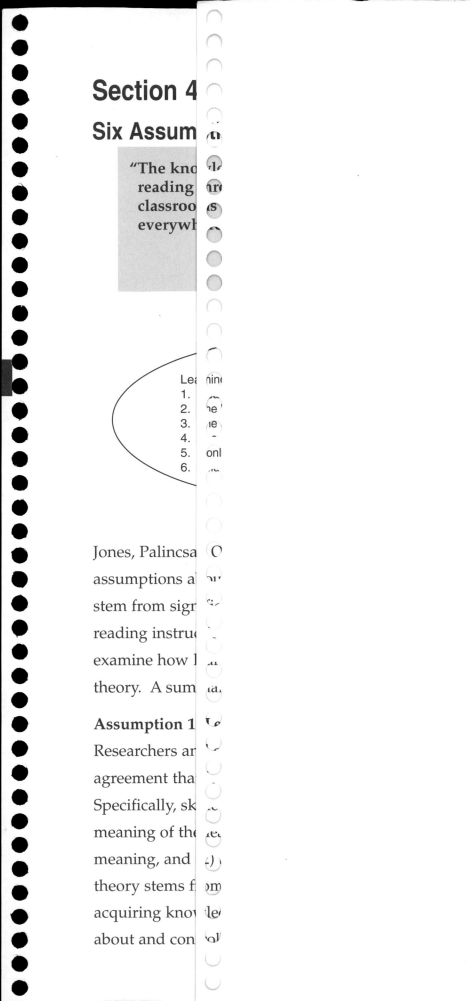

Section 4

Six Assum...

> "The kno...
> reading...
> classroo...
> everywh...

Lea...ning
1.
2. he
3. ie
4.
5. onl
6.

Jones, Palincsa...
assumptions a...
stem from sign...
reading instruc...
examine how I...
theory. A sum...

Assumption 1
Researchers ar...
agreement tha...
Specifically, sk...
meaning of the...
meaning, and...
theory stems fr...om
acquiring know...le
about and con...

Six Assumptions
about Learning

Although most educators are aware of the importance of constructing meaning and self-directed learning, this approach is relatively new. Previous theories of learning held that learning was essentially a matter of responding to information provided by an outside source, like a teacher or textbook. Reading was considered a passive activity as well, involving little more than decoding words on the page. Cognitive psychologists now maintain that learning is thinking—the active construction of meaning by the learner.

The landmark document, *Becoming a Nation of Readers* (Anderson, Hiebert, Scott, and Wilkinson, 1985), reviews reading research and depicts the ideal reader as active, strategic, and constructive in linking new information to background knowledge. Thus, we have experienced a remarkable change in our approach to learning and reading: We now conceptualize both as dependent on prior knowledge and on the application of specific strategies to construct meaning and understand ideas in a text.

Assumption 2: Learning is the linking of new information to prior knowledge.

Learning theorists posit that one's prior knowledge and past experience are stored in memory banks called

> "Better learning will not come from finding better ways for the teacher to instruct but from giving the learner better opportunities to construct."
>
> **Seymour Papert**
> Author of *Mindstorms* and *The Children's Machine*

schemata. Schemata are mental maps, or frameworks, that provide a structure or guide for understanding. Schemata are not distinct; rather, they are highly interrelated and significantly impact comprehension. A reader's schema (the singular form of schemata) comprises the total amount of knowledge she has about a given subject. Her schema allows her to:

- seek and select important information;
- make inferences;
- develop predictions;

- organize what is read;
- elaborate on, judge, and evaluate text (Vacca and Vacca, 1993).

Accessing prior knowledge is not always an easy task. Various factors can obstruct a learner's use of prior knowledge. For example, if information in the text is unclear, disorganized, or does not make sense to the reader, he may experience difficulty calling up relevant prior knowledge. Also, one's purpose for reading will influence how he uses prior knowledge to make connections while reading; this, in turn, affects comprehension. In one study, students told to read a description of a house as if they were home buyers were able to recall the location and number of bathrooms, while students who were told to read the passage from the perspective of a burglar remembered information about security systems and the number and location of windows (Jones, Palincsar, Ogle, and Carr; 1987).

Students may have difficulty activating prior knowledge if that knowledge is what some researchers term "inert knowledge"— knowledge students have but can't access because they lack the appropriate strategies that help learners retrieve what they know (Bransford, Sherwood, Vye, and Rieser; 1986). Many learning strategies in this manual can help students access necessary information.

Assumption 3: Learning involves organizing information.
The ideal reader knows different ways to organize information. She understands different organizational patterns in text and can impose patterns while reading. Thus, a knowledge of organizational patterns can exist both "inside the head" as a conceptual framework and also "outside the head" in printed text. Knowledge of text structure and organizational patterns helps the reader:

1. find information in the text.
2. distinguish between what is important and what is less important.

3. integrate and synthesize information gleaned from within particular text or from various texts.

4. impose organization on relatively unorganized information.

5. revise and restructure existing schema.

Text type and purpose often determine organizational structure. Narrative text, written primarily to entertain, is commonly organized in sequential or chronological order. Fiction novels, short stories, and biographies are examples of narrative text. In contrast, informational text is written to inform or persuade. Authors of informational text select from a number of organizational patterns to express the relationships among their important and less-important ideas. In this manual we present seven organizational patterns. Each has its own distinctive characteristics that appear across content areas:

1. Chronological sequence

2. Comparison and contrast

3. Concept/definition

4. Description

5. Episode

6. Generalization/principle

7. Process/cause-effect

Anderson and Armbruster (1984) suggest that textbook organization can be viewed as either *considerate* or *inconsiderate*. Considerate text is easier to read because it is well-organized and clearly written. Signal words cue readers to the author's organizational plan, and ideas appear in a logical sequence. In contrast, inconsiderate text is difficult to read because it is poorly organized and poorly written: The organization of ideas does not match the author's purpose; the sentence structure may be complicated; the vocabulary may be too difficult for the intended audience.

Current cognitive research indicates that the use of frames and graphic organizers can enhance comprehension and recall of text material. Graphic organizers provide a visual representation of facts and concepts, and how these are related. Semantic maps, flow charts, webs or mind maps, and matrices can be used to represent text information graphically.

Assumption 4: Learning is the acquisition of cognitive and metacognitive structures.

Strategic learners are aware of their learning style and are able to select and regulate their use of learning skills and strategies. Skills are mental activities learners apply to the task of learning, such as activating prior knowledge, summarizing and making predictions. Strategies are specific procedures or tools one uses to perform a skill. Using an anticipation guide is a strategy one can employ to activate prior knowledge.

Skilled learners not only know specific learning strategies but also know how and when to use them. For instance, when a student recognizes that his method of determining the meaning of a word from context isn't working, he perseveres until he finds another strategy that will help. He realizes that he is in control of his learning and is motivated to find a strategy that will work. He is skillful and self-disciplined about learning.

Assumption 5: Learning occurs in phases, yet is nonlinear.
Researchers believe that learning has three phases:

- Phase 1: Preactive thought or preparing for learning
- Phase 2: Interactive thought or processing that occurs during the actual learning
- Phase 3: Reflective thought to integrate, extend, refine, and apply what has been learned

(Costa and Garmston, 1994; Buehl, 1995)

The preactive phase sets the stage for learning. During this phase the learner prepares for learning by activating prior knowledge. She previews that text to learn its organizational structure and to determine what subject-specific reading skills might be needed. She may skim the text, prewrite about the topic, or mentally review what she knows. During this phase the learner also identifies her purpose for reading and selects a reading style that will help her stay focused and achieve her purpose.

During the interactive phase, learners are actively engaged in processing what they read. They select what they think is most important, and they undertake some method to organize this information. They evaluate their earlier predictions and hypotheses in light of new information read, revising them as needed. What Jones, Palincsar, Ogle, and Carr term the "start-pause" nature of the learning process is especially evident during this phase. That is, readers monitor their comprehension and adjust their progress, sometimes looking back over material for clarification, or developing a mental summary of what was read and evaluating new information in light of prior knowledge. Thus, while learning occurs in phases, it is not a neatly linear process.

Reflective thought is an integral part of learning. Model readers reflect on what they read, and this reflection helps them to deepen their understanding of the text as a whole. Reflection also helps readers to synthesize what they have read and to integrate new learning into their existing schema.

Assumption 6: Learning is influenced by cognitive development.

Not all children arrive at school equally prepared or ready to understand printed text. Some children may have acquired more preliteracy skills or prior knowledge than others. However, all students can be taught to use thinking and learning strategies. Furthermore, strategy instruction is imperative for low-achieving students who are not likely to develop effective cognitive and metacognitive strategies on their own. These students need numerous opportunities to practice and apply these skills and to obtain corrective feedback.

One final note about strategy instruction: If students already have an efficient strategy for learning a skill or given type of content, teachers should allow them to continue using that strategy rather than require that they learn a new one. Research suggests that for these students, explicit strategy instruction may actually hinder their learning.

Reading Strategies

Section 5

Reading Strategies

Vocabulary Development

1. Concept Definition Mapping

What is it?

Concept Definition Mapping (Schwartz,1988) is a strategy for teaching students the meaning of key concepts. Concept Definition Maps are graphic organizers that help students understand the essential attributes, qualities, or characteristics of a word's meaning. Students must describe what the concept is, as well as what it isn't, and cite examples of it. Looking up the concept's definition in the dictionary is not nearly as effective as this process, which gives students a more thorough understanding of what the concept means, includes, and implies. The mapping process also aids recall.

How to use it:

1. Using a flip chart or overhead transparency, display an example of a concept definition map.

2. Discuss the questions that a definition should answer:

   - What is it? What broader category or classification of things does it fit into?

   - What is it like? What are its essential characteristics? What qualities does it possess that make it different from other things in the same category?

   - What are some examples of it?

3. Model how to use the map by selecting a familiar vocabulary term from a previous unit and mapping its features.

4. Select another familiar vocabulary term, and have students volunteer information for a map. For instance, a science teacher might choose the concept *migration.* "What is it like?" responses might include "seasonal," "movement from one area to another," "animals looking for food and favorable climate to raise their young." Examples could include Canadian geese, whales, monarch butterflies, and elk.

McREL

Vocabulary Development

5. Have students work in pairs to complete a map for a concept in their current unit of study. They may choose to use a dictionary or glossary, but encourage them to use their own experience and background knowledge as well.

6. After students complete their maps, instruct them to write a complete definition of the concept, using the information from their maps.

7. As a unit progresses, encourage students to refine their maps as they learn additional characteristics and examples of the concept.

Examples of Visual Representations: **Concept Map**

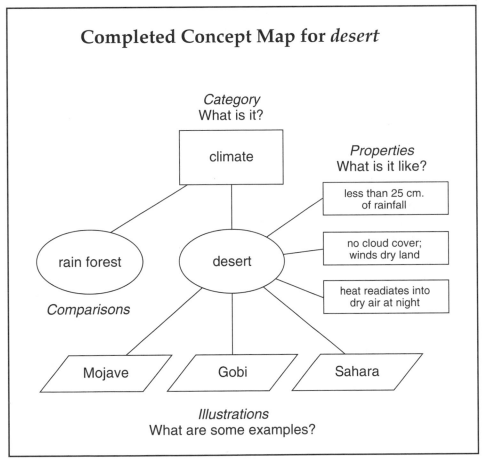

Completed Concept Map for *desert*

Category
What is it?

climate

Properties
What is it like?

less than 25 cm. of rainfall

rain forest

desert

no cloud cover; winds dry land

Comparisons

heat readiates into dry air at night

Mojave

Gobi

Sahara

Illustrations
What are some examples?

Note: From "Learning to learn vocabulary in content area textbooks," by R.M. Schwartz, 1988, in *Journal of Reading*, p.113. Copyright © 1988 by the International Reading Association. Reprinted with permission.

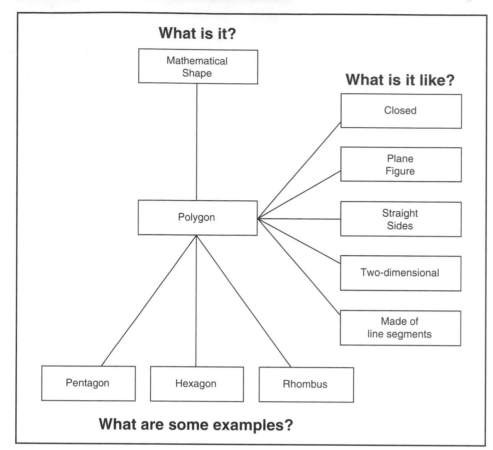

What is it?

Mathematical Shape

What is it like?

Closed

Plane Figure

Straight Sides

Two-dimensional

Made of line segments

Polygon

Pentagon

Hexagon

Rhombus

What are some examples?

Note: From "Concept of definition: a key to improving students' vocabulary," by R. Schwartz and T. Raphael, 1985, in *The Reading Teacher, 39* (2). Copyright © 1985 by the International Reading Association. Reprinted with permission.

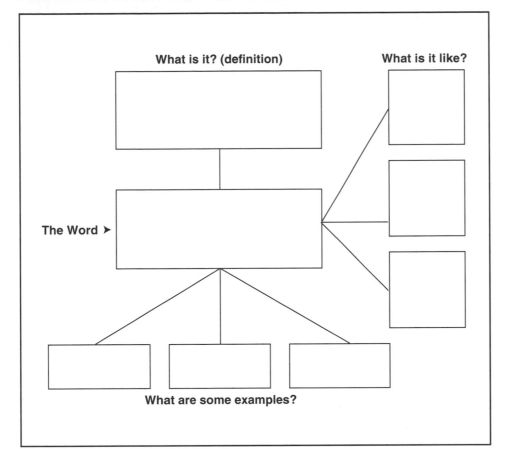

What is it? (definition)

What is it like?

The Word ➤

What are some examples?

Note: From "Concept of definition: a key to improving students' vocabulary," by R. Schwartz and T. Raphael, 1985, in *The Reading Teacher, 39* (2). Copyright © 1985 by the International Reading Association. Reprinted with permission.

Vocabulary Development

2. Frayer Model

What is it?

The Frayer Model (Frayer, Frederick, & Klausmeier, 1969) is a word categorization activity. Frayer believes learners develop their understanding of concepts by studying them in a relational manner. Using the Frayer model, students analyze a word's essential and nonessential attributes and also refine their understanding by choosing examples and non-examples of the concept. In order to understand completely what a concept is, one must also know what it isn't. The "Four Square" version of the model works well with younger children.

How to use it:

1. Assign the concept or word being studied.

2. Explain all of the attributes of the Frayer Model to be completed.

3. Using an easy word such as *polygon*, complete the model with the class.

4. Have students work in pairs and complete their model diagram using the assigned concept or word.

5. Once the diagram is complete, have students share their work with other students. If students develop the diagram on chart paper with colored markers, display the posters during the entire unit of study so that students can refer to the words being studied. Students can continue to add ideas to displayed models.

McREL

Examples of Visual Representations: **Frayer Model**

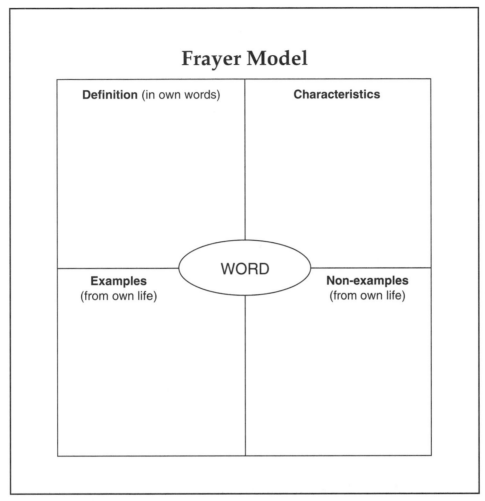

Frayer Model

Definition (in own words)	Characteristics
Examples (from own life)	WORD	Non-examples (from own life)

Note: **From "A schema for testing the level of concept mastery," 1969, by D.A. Frayer, W.C. Frederick, and H.G. Klausmeier, in** *Technical Report No. 16,* **Copyright © 1969 by the University of Wisconsin.**

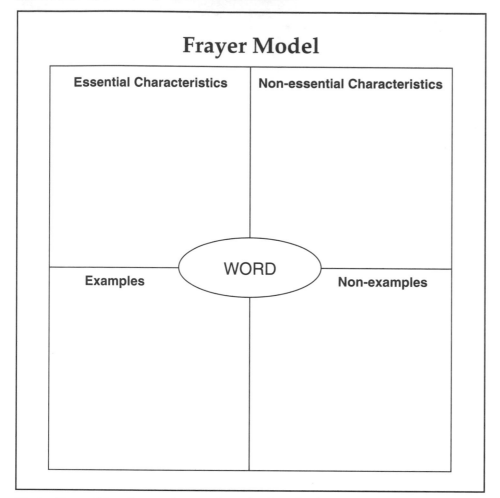

Frayer Model

Essential Characteristics	Non-essential Characteristics

WORD

Examples	Non-examples

Note: From "A schema for testing the level of concept mastery," 1969, by D.A. Frayer, W.C. Frederick, and H.G. Klausmeier, in *Technical Report No. 16*, Copyright © 1969 by the University of Wisconsin.

McREL

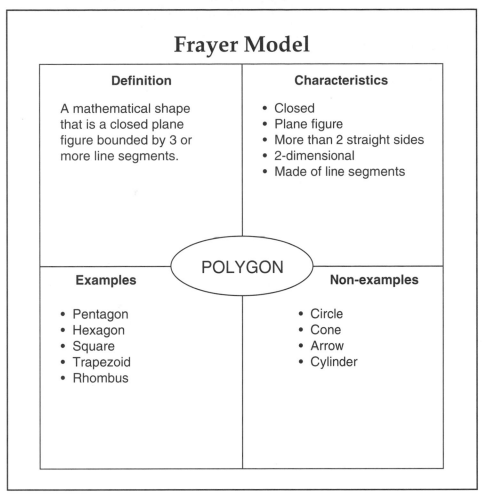

Frayer Model

Definition

A mathematical shape that is a closed plane figure bounded by 3 or more line segments.

Characteristics

- Closed
- Plane figure
- More than 2 straight sides
- 2-dimensional
- Made of line segments

POLYGON

Examples

- Pentagon
- Hexagon
- Square
- Trapezoid
- Rhombus

Non-examples

- Circle
- Cone
- Arrow
- Cylinder

Note: From "A schema for testing the level of concept mastery," 1969, by D.A. Frayer, W.C. Frederick, and H.G. Klausmeier, in *Technical Report No. 16,* Copyright © 1969 by the University of Wisconsin.

Vocabulary Development

3. Prereading Predictions

What is it?

Prereading Predictions is useful for activating prior knowledge and making predictions about story content. In addition, teachers can use the strategy to have students analyze correct usage and effective word choice.

How to use it:

1. Before students read a story, the teacher selects approximately twenty to thirty colorful, unusual, and/or unfamiliar vocabulary words used by the author. The teacher lists these terms in columns, grouping them by parts of speech; that is, all of the nouns are listed in one column, verbs in another, and so on. Each student examines this list of words, and depending upon developmental level, may work in small groups or as a class to review the meanings of any familiar terms and to make some guesses about unfamiliar words' meanings.

2. Next, the teacher models for students a few ways the words in different columns might be combined to form simple sentences. The teacher asks students to explain which combinations "make sense," which do not, and why.

3. Based on the lists, students are asked to predict what the story might be about.

4. After reading the story, students revisit their lists and identify how the author actually used these words. At this point, the teacher may encourage students to discuss why the author might have chosen those words to tell the story, whether the students would have chosen different words than the author did, and what effect wording can have on a story's meaning and mood.

Vocabulary Development

4. Semantic Feature Analysis

What is it?

Semantic Feature Analysis (Baldwin, Ford, & Readance, 1981; Johnson & Pearson, 1984) helps students discern a term's meaning by comparing its features to those of other terms that fall into the same category or class. When students have completed a semantic feature matrix, they have a visual reminder of how certain terms are alike or different. Students find that the matrix provides a good summary of concept features and helps in reviewing for exams.

How to use it:

1. Select a general category of study. With younger students, choose concrete concepts such as sports, food, farm animals, or board games. As students become adept at using this model, they can analyze more sophisticated or abstract categories such as geometric forms, literary movements, forms of government, economic cycles, or land forms.

2. Create a matrix: along the left side, list key vocabulary terms or concepts within the chosen category. These should be familiar to the students. Across the top of the matrix, supply features that these words might share.

3. Students then use an "X" to indicate if the feature applies to the vocabulary word. An alternative is marking a plus sign (+) if the feature applies or a minus sign (-) if it does not. If students mark the exact same pattern of pluses and minuses, or Xs, for more than one word, challenge them to identify a feature that will differentiate between these terms.

4. Students are encouraged to explain to other students the rationale behind their markings. Explaining their reasoning and listening to others' reasons enhances understanding of the concepts.

5. As the unit progresses and understanding of each term deepens, the teacher or students can add terms and features to the matrix. In each case, understanding deepens as students examine the terms' similarities and differences. Guide students in developing generalizations about how each concept is unique in relation to the other semantically-related vocabulary terms.

Examples of Visual Representation: **Semantic Feature Analysis**

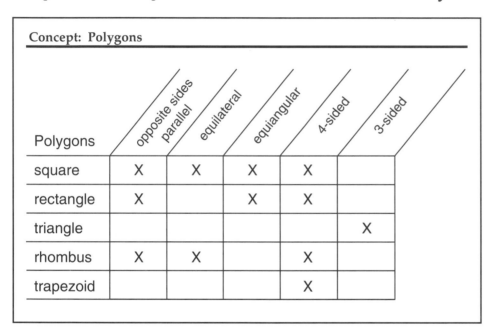

Concept: **Polygons**

Polygons	opposite sides parallel	equilateral	equiangular	4-sided	3-sided
square	X	X	X	X	
rectangle	X		X	X	
triangle					X
rhombus	X	X		X	
trapezoid				X	

Concept: Heroes in Literature

Heroes	noble demi-god	human with super-human abilities	common man whose values and insights are admirable	anti-hero	tragic figure
Achilles	x				
Billy Budd			x		x
Huck Finn			x		
Paul Bunyan		x	x		
Willy Loman				x	x

Vocabulary Development

5. Semantic Mapping

What is it?

A semantic map is a visual tool that helps readers activate and draw on prior knowledge, recognize important components of different concepts, and see the relationships among these components.

How to use it:

1. Write the subject of the lesson in the middle of the chalk board.

2. Encourage students to think of as many words as possible that relate in some way to that term. This can be done as a brainstorming session completed by the class, or students can develop lists on their own.

3. Have students write down these words. In small groups, or individually if students created their own lists, students then group the terms into categories and depict these categories in the form of a map or web.

4. Students share their semantic maps with the class, explaining the reasoning behind their categories and the words they have grouped under each. Discussion of the semantic map is an essential part of the lesson. As they listen and share, students become aware of new words, gather new meanings for familiar terms, and see relationships among numerous words associated with the lesson.

McREL

Vocabulary Development

Examples of Visual Representation: **Semantic Maps**

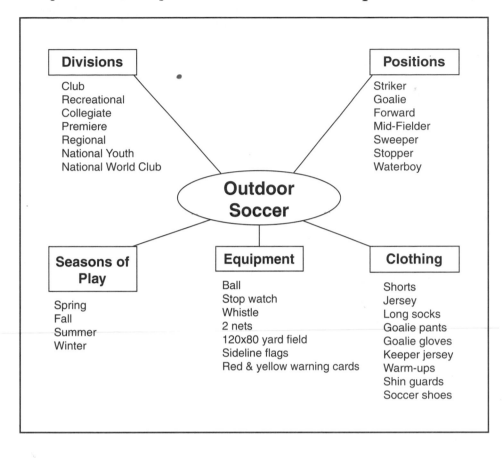

Divisions

Club
Recreational
Collegiate
Premiere
Regional
National Youth
National World Club

Positions

Striker
Goalie
Forward
Mid-Fielder
Sweeper
Stopper
Waterboy

Outdoor Soccer

Seasons of Play

Spring
Fall
Summer
Winter

Equipment

Ball
Stop watch
Whistle
2 nets
120x80 yard field
Sideline flags
Red & yellow warning cards

Clothing

Shorts
Jersey
Long socks
Goalie pants
Goalie gloves
Keeper jersey
Warm-ups
Shin guards
Soccer shoes

McREL

Vocabulary Development

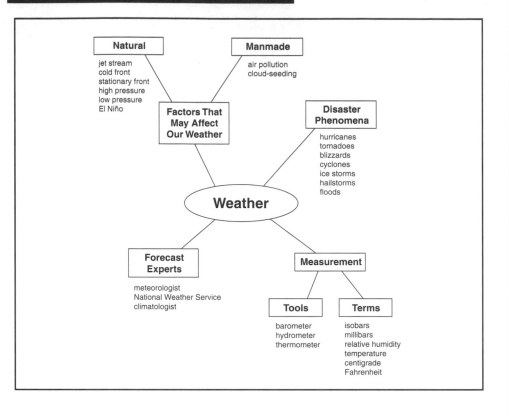

84

Vocabulary Development

6. Stephens Vocabulary Elaboration Strategy (SVES)

What is it?

The Stephens Vocabulary Elaboration Strategy (Brown, Phillips, & Stephens, 1993) illustrates how vocabulary meanings can vary in different social contexts, content areas, and time periods. Students maintain a "living" vocabulary notebook in which they record unfamiliar terms, their definitions, and a description of each term's usage and meaning every time they encounter it.

How to use it:

The authors explain how to use the strategy in the box below.

Stephens Vocabulary Elaboration Strategy
How to Use It

Led by Teacher or Done in Collaborative Learning Groups

A. Initial Encounter with Word (or Phrase)
  1. Write word and date first encountered.
  2. Describe context of initial encounter.
  3. Explore, discuss, and begin to formulate a definition related to that context.
  4. List examples generated from personal experiences and prior knowledge.
  5. List non-examples generated from personal experiences and prior knowledge to show what the word is not or how it differs from other closely related words.
  6. Write a definition in your own words; compare with dictionary or glossary.
  7. Develop appropriate graphic organizers, such as word maps, attribute charts, and compare/contrast diagrams.
  8. Create visual association drawings, if appropriate.

B. Additional Encounters with Word
  1. Write additional date(s) encountered.
  2. Describe context of new encounter and compare with previous contexts.
  3. Explore, discuss, and begin to formulate a definition in new context(s) and relate to previous definition(s).
  4. Add to, revise, and elaborate on work done in steps 4, 5, 6, 7, and 8, listed under Initial Encounter.

Note: **From *Toward literacy: theory and applications for teaching writing in the content areas*, by A.L. Brown, L.B. Phillips, and E.C. Stephens, 1993, Belmont, CA: Wadsworth. Copyright © 1993 Wadsworth Publishing Inc. Reprinted with permission.**

Vocabulary Development

Examples of Visual Representation: **SVES**

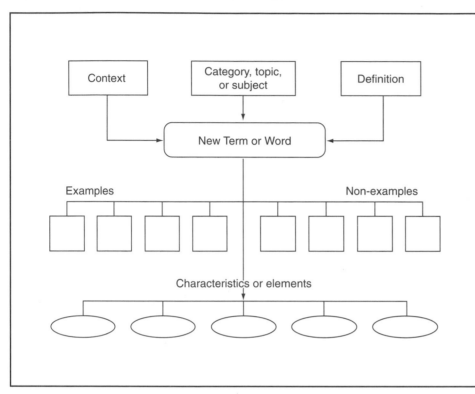

Note: From *Toward literacy: theory and applications for teaching writing in the content areas*, by A.L. Brown, L.B. Phillips, and E.C. Stephens, 1993, Belmont, CA: Wadsworth. Copyright © 1993 Wadsworth Publishing Inc. Reprinted with permission.

McREL

Vocabulary Development

7. Student VOC Strategy

What is it?

The Student VOC Strategy is useful for helping students analyze word meanings from context. The strategy also allows students to make meaningful sensory connections that relate to their particular learning style. When students write their definitions for the terms and then make a sensory connection with it, they are engaged in a "whole" brain activity that increases retention.

How to use it:

1. Students are assigned a passage to read.

2. Key vocabulary words, written on the chalkboard or chart, are shared with the students prior to reading.

3. The students are directed to identify unfamiliar terms on the list and to learn their meanings by using the VOC strategy:

    • Write the actual sentence in which the word appears.

    •. Based on how the word is used in that sentence, write down a prediction about its meaning.

    • Consult an "expert" for the actual definition: ask a friend who is familiar with the word, ask a teacher its meaning, or use another resource. Write down that definition.

    • Show your understanding of the word's meaning by using it in a sentence of your own.

    • Choose one of the following ways to help you remember the word's meaning: draw a picture of what the word means to you; select and perform a miming action that the word reminds you of; or connect the word with something similar that you've heard—a story, a news report, a song.

Vocabulary Development

- Below the sentence you created, write down the association or connection you have made.

- Finally, explain to a partner your understanding of the word's meaning as well as the visual, mental, or physical representation you chose that will help you recall that definition.

Examples of Visual Representation: **Student VOC Strategy**

Vocabulary Word: _____

1. Write the sentence in which it appears in the text:

_____

_____

2. Based upon how it is used in the text, predict what the word means:

_____

3. Consult an "expert" for the actual definition (e.g., a friend, teacher, text resource).   Expert: _____

Expert's definition: _____

_____

4. Show your understanding of the word by using it in a sentence of your own: _____

_____

_____

5. Choose one of the following ways to help you remember the word's meaning: draw a picture of what the word means to you; select and perform a miming action that the word reminds you of; or connect the word with something similar that you've heard—a story, a news report, a song. Below the sentence you created, write down the association or connection you have made:

_____

6. Explain why you chose this way to represent what the word means to you:

_____

_____

Vocabulary Development

8. Word Sorts

What is it?

Word sorts (Gillett & Temple, 1983) help students recognize the semantic relationships among key concepts. Students are asked to sort vocabulary terms into different categories. The strategy can be used in two different ways. In a "closed sort," the teacher provides the categories into which students are to assign the words. In an "open sort," students group words into categories and identify their own labels for each category. Word sorts help students develop a deeper understanding of key concepts, and also are an excellent method of teaching the complex reasoning skills of classification and deduction.

How to use it:

1. Students copy vocabulary terms onto 3"x 5" cards, one word per card.

2. Individually or in groups, students then sort the words into categories. With younger students or complex concepts, the teacher should provide students with the categories and have students complete a "closed sort."

3. As students become more proficient at classifying, teachers should ask them to complete "open sorts"; that is, students sort words into labeled categories of their own making. At this stage, students should be encouraged to find more than one way to classify the vocabulary terms. Classifying and then reclassifying helps students extend and refine their understanding of the concepts studied.

9. Character Map

What is it?

One good way to better understand the characters in a story is to make a character map. The visual image created by such a drawing enhances understanding and promotes retention.

How to use it:

1. Read the story.

2. Draw a simple picture of the character of interest.

3. Near the picture, make four or five lines for writing what the character does or say.

4. Make a long line beneath the picture for writing a sentence that tells what kinds of person the character is.

Examples of Visual Representations: **Character Maps**

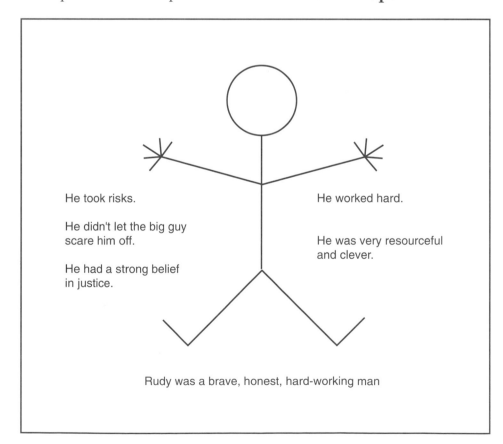

He took risks.

He didn't let the big guy scare him off.

He had a strong belief in justice.

He worked hard.

He was very resourceful and clever.

Rudy was a brave, honest, hard-working man

Character Map

Now it's your turn!

Practice making a character map of

- a friend
- a loved one
- your principal
- other

10. Directed Reading/Thinking Activity (DR/TA)

What is it?

Directed Reading/Thinking Activity (Stauffer, 1969) is a versatile activity that gives students practice in active reading skills. It involves 3 processes: predicting, reading, and proving.

How to use it:

1. Tell students to preview the story, prereading the title, noting any subtitles and pictures, and reading the introductory paragraph.

2. Ask students to predict what they think will happen in the story, based on this preview.

3. After making these predictions, students read to a place in the story that makes a logical break in the action.

4. When students have finished reading to that point, lead a discussion on the accuracy of their predictions. Students then make new predictions about what they think will happen in the rest of the story, using references to the story to defend their hypotheses. Point out that active readers engage in a mental dialogue with the author, making predictions, revising them, making new predictions, etc.

5. Repeat this process when students are finished reading, and ask students to summarize what they learned from engaging in this predict-read-prove process.

Narrative Text

11. Probable Passages

What is it?

Probable Passages (Wood, 1988) is a pre-reading technique that integrates prediction, summarization, vocabulary instruction, and story frames.

How to use it:

1. Select important terms and concepts from a story to be read.

2. Have the students categorize them according to the story elements of setting, characters, problems, events, and resolution. (See p. 94.) Then have each student write a probable story by using the words in each category and a frame similar to the following:

```
The story takes place _____.

_____ is a character who _____.

A problem occurs when _____.

The problem is solved when _____.

The story ends when _____.
```

Note: **From "Guiding students through informational text," by K. Wood, 1988, in *The Reading Teacher*, 41(9). Copyright © 1988 by the International Reading Association. Reprinted with permission.**

3. Have the students read the story and compare it to the version they predicted. Then have the students modify their predicted story to make it a summary paragraph.

MᴄREL

Examples of Visual Representations: **Probable Passages**

Probable Passages: A Reading-Writing Strategy

Setting	Characters	Problem	Problem-Solution	Ending

Note: Adapted from "Guiding students through informational text," by K. Wood, 1988, in *The Reading Teacher, 41*(9). Copyright © 1988 by the International Reading Association. Reprinted with permission.

Narrative Text

12. Story Frame

What is it?

Completing a Story Frame (Fowler, 1982) such as the graphic below can help the reader organize and examine the logical progression and sequence of events in a story. Teachers can use this strategy to discuss the causal nature and structure of narrative text.

Story Frame

In this story, the problem starts when _____

_____

After that _____

_____

Next, _____

_____

Then, _____

_____

The problem is finally solved when_____

_____

The story ends with _____

_____

Note: **From "Developing comprehension skills in primary students through the use of story frames," by G.L. Fowler, 1982, in** *The Reading Teacher, 36* **(2). Copyright © 1982 by the International Reading Association. Reprinted with permission.**

How to use it:

1. Present the story frame to students before reading the story.

2. Read the frame with learners, noting the blank spaces they are supposed to complete.

3. Ask learners to read the story.

4. Ask learners to complete the story frame independently, using information from the story.

5. After learners complete the story frame, help students evaluate how well they captured the major plot events. Depending on the developmental level of the students, lead a discussion on the cause-effect pattern in narrative text, and whether the plot developed logically and realistically.

Narrative Text

13. Story Grammar/Maps

What is it?

Story grammar identifies the story's structure, literary elements, and their relationship to one another. A Story Map (Beck & McKeown, 1981) is a visual representation of the story structure. Students find graphic organizers like the ones that follow helpful in sequencing and explaining the elements of different narrative text.

How to use it:

1. The teacher constructs a Story Map outline, and the students fill in the specific information after reading the story selection.

2. Students may construct their own Story Maps using the necessary story elements.

3. Story Maps might be shared and discussed in small groups.

Examples of Visual Representations: **Story Maps**

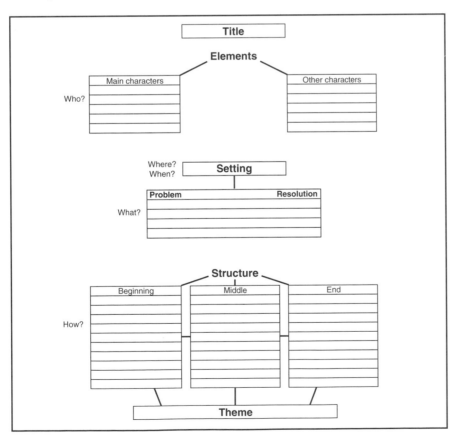

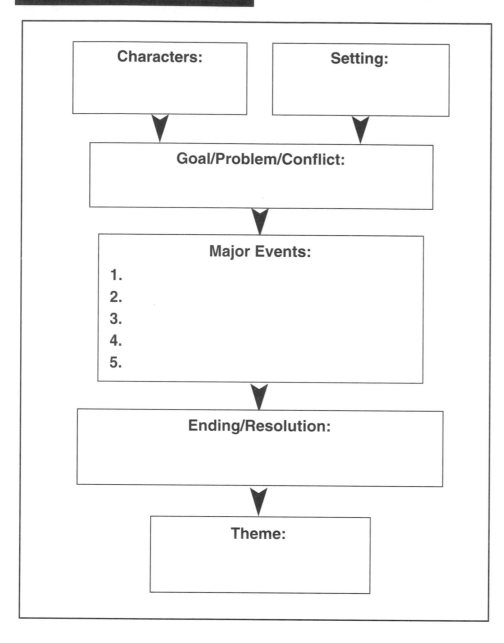

Characters:

Setting:

Goal/Problem/Conflict:

Major Events:
1.
2.
3.
4.
5.

Ending/Resolution:

Theme:

Narrative Text

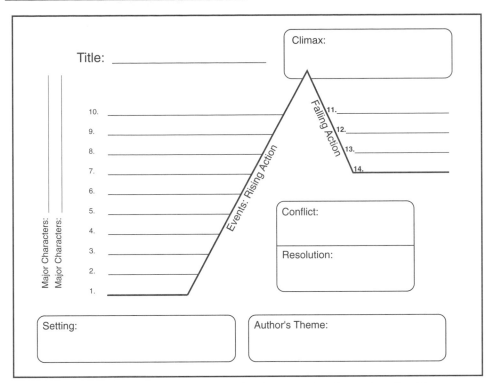

Note: From *Classroom strategies for interactive learning,* by Doug Buehl, 1995, Schofield, WI: Wisconsin State Reading Association. Copyright © 1995 by the Wisconsin State Reading Association. Reprinted with permission.

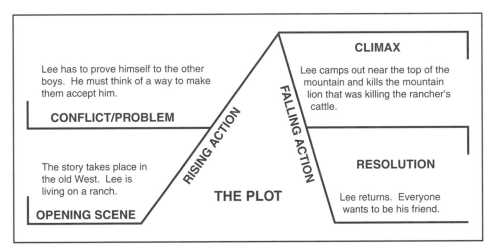

Note: From *Strengthening student learning by applying the latest research on the brain to your classroom teaching,* by M. Sorgen and P. Wolfe, 1998, Bellevue, WA: Bureau of Education & Research. Copyright © 1998 Bureau of Education & Research. Reprinted with permission.

McREL

14. Story Mapping Through Circular Pictures

What is it?

Because story mapping (Routman, 1991) requires readers to draw sketches or pictures of the main events in a story in chronological order, this strategy functions as both a graphic organizer and a mnemonic device.

How to use it:

1. After reading a story or book, ask the students to draw a brief sketch of the beginning of the story at the top of the page.

2. Ask the students to continue drawing the main events of the story in a clockwise fashion until the circle is complete.

3. Ask the students to explain their decisions about the main events.

4. Have students share their circular story maps with one another, comparing their ideas and sketches.

Narrative Text

Examples of Visual Representations: **Story Mapping Through Circular Pictures**

Story Mapping offers learners a visual representaion of the events in a story, in the order that they occurred.

1. After reading a story or book, ask the learners to draw a brief sketch of the beginning of the story as indicated below.

2. Ask learners to continue drawing the main events of the story in a clockwise fashion. At least six events should be depicted.

3. Ask the learners to explain their decisions about main events.

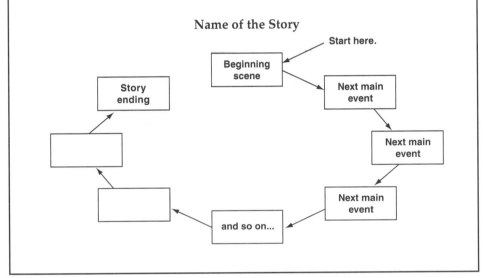

Name of the Story

Adapted from Routmann, 1991.

15. Venn Diagram

What is it?

A Venn diagram requires the learner to compare and contrast two items being studied. Learners can use a Venn Diagram to compare two books, two versions of a story, or a story told in two different mediums, such as a book or a videotape.

How to use it:

1. Draw two interconnecting circles. Above each circle, label the medium that will have ideas listed in that circle.

2. Present the Venn diagram to the students before reading the story.

3. Discuss the Venn diagram with learners, noting the items they will compare and contrast.

4. Ask learners to read the story.

5. Ask learners to complete the Venn diagram independently, using information from the story.

6. After learners complete the Venn diagram, have them share the diagrams with each other and explain their thinking.

Narrative Text

Examples of Visual Representations: **Venn Diagram**

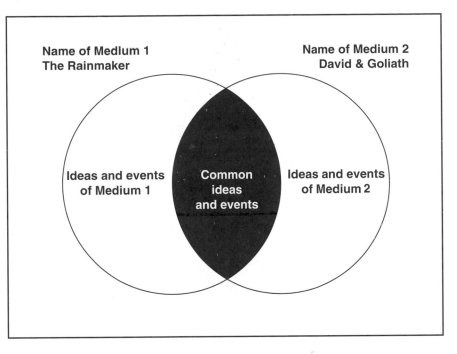

Informational Text

16. Anticipation Guide/Prediction Guide

What is it?

Anticipation/prediction guides (Herber, 1978) can be used to activate and assess students' prior knowledge, to focus reading, and to motivate reluctant readers by stimulating their interest in the topic. Because the guide revolves around the text's most important concepts, students are prepared to focus on and pay attention to this information while reading. Students are motivated to read closely in order to search for evidence that supports their answers and predictions. Consequently, these guides promote active reading and critical thinking. Anticipation guides are especially useful in identifying any misperceptions students have so that the teacher can correct these prior to reading.

How to use it:

1. Identify the major concepts that you want students to learn from reading.

2. Determine ways these concepts might support or challenge the students' beliefs.

3. Create four to six statements that support or challenge the students' beliefs and experiences about the topic under study. The statements can address important points, major concepts, controversial ideas, or misconceptions. Do not write simple, literal statements that can be easily answered.

4. Share the guide with students. Ask the students to react to each statement, formulate a response to it, and be prepared to defend their opinions. Students can work in groups if the subject matter is fairly complex, or you can ask students to fill in their answers on their own.

5. Discuss each statement with the class. Ask how many students agreed or disagreed with each statement. Ask one student from each side of the issue to explain his response.

McREL

6. Have students read the selection with the purpose of finding evidence that supports or disconfirms their responses on the guide.

7. After students finish reading the selection, have them confirm their original responses, revise them, or decide what additional information is needed. Students may be encouraged to rewrite any statement that was not true in a way that makes it true.

8. Lead a discussion on what students learned from their reading.

Examples of Visual Representations: **Anticipation Guides**

Anticipation Guide
(Elementary Science Unit on the Heart)

Directions: In the column labeled *me,* place a check next to any statement with which you agree. After reading the text, compare your opinions on those statements with information contained in the text.

Me Text

_____ _____ 1. Your heart is the size of your fist.

_____ _____ 2. The heart is divided into six (6) sections.

_____ _____ 3. The heart rate is the same as the pulse rate.

_____ _____ 4. The heart is a muscle.

_____ _____ 5. The heart pumps blood to the lungs before it pumps blood to the rest of the body.

Anticipation Guide
(Language Arts Example)

Animal Farm

Directions: In the column labeled *me,* place a check next to any statement with which you tend to agree. Be prepared to defend and support your opinions with specific examples. After reading *Animal Farm,* place a check next to those statements with which you think George Orwell would agree.

Me	George Orwell	
_____	_____	It is a good idea to be distrustful of political leaders.
_____	_____	Those who work harder than others should be paid more.
_____	_____	When someone is unable to work, s/he should be supported by the government.
_____	_____	People are generally motivated by self-interest.
_____	_____	Power eventually corrupts those who have it.

Anticipation Guide
(Social Studies Example)

The Ku Klux Klan

Directions: In the column labeled *me,* place a check next to any statement with which you tend to agree. Be prepared to defend and support your opinions with specific examples.

After reading the text, compare your opinions on those statements with those of the author. At that time, check those statements with which the author would agree.

Me	Author		
_____	_____	1.	The Ku Klux Klan (KKK) was founded in the 1900s.
_____	_____	2.	The KKK has terrorized not only African Americans, but Jews, Catholics, and union organizers.
_____	_____	3.	A number of high-ranking politicians have been members of the KKK.
_____	_____	4.	Any group, even the Klan, should be allowed to voice its beliefs through meetings, publications, and protest marches.
_____	_____	5.	Groups such as the Klan become more powerful because they appeal to people's fear and mistrust.

Informational Text

17. DR/TA (Directed Reading/Thinking Activity)

What is it?

The Directed Reading/Thinking Activity (Stauffer, 1969) is similar to K-W-L in both concept and versatility. It encourages active reading through activation of prior knowledge, predicting, and checking the accuracy of predictions.

How to use it:

1. Have students preview the text selection, noting the title, any subheadings, and graphic aids. From this preview, students may complete the first three sections of the DR/TA form. That is, they should write down what they know about the subject of the selection, what they think may be true about it, and what they think they will learn from closer reading of the text. The first two sections help students focus on the topic. Discussing these sections can also expose any misperceptions students have about the topic. The third section requires students to formulate hypotheses or predictions about what they will read, which sets the purpose for reading.

2. Have students read the text selection, confirming or rejecting their earlier hypotheses about the subject matter, and refining their hypotheses as new information is gathered.

3. Students conclude their reading by completing the last section of the form, "What do you know you learned?" This helps to reinforce understanding and to revise schema.

Example of Visual Representations: **DR/TA**

Directed Reading/Thinking Activity

What I know I know:

What I think I know:

What I think I'll learn:

What I know I learned:

Informational Text

18. Graphic Organizers

What is it?

Graphic organizers provide a visual, holistic representation of facts and concepts and also the relationships that link them together. They are effective tools for thinking and learning as they help students to

- Represent abstract ideas in more concrete forms.
- Depict the relationships among facts and concepts.
- Organize ideas.
- Store and recall information.

The web, also known as a mind map or concept map, is the most widely used example of a graphic organizer.

How to use it:

1. Explain the purpose and benefits of using graphic organizers:
   - the importance of organizing information
   - how using a visual organizer can aid retention, comprehension, and recall
2. Introduce a specific graphic organizer by describing its
   - purpose (e.g., a mind map for making a creative outline)
   - form (e.g., a center circle with straight lines extending from it)
3. Explain and model how to use the selected organizer with
   - familiar information
   - new information
4. Let students apply the graphic organizer to
   - familiar material
   - new material

5. Have students reflect on what they liked about using the graphic organizer and how they might adapt it for use in other contexts.

6. Provide multiple opportunities for the students to practice using the graphic organizer.

7. Encourage students to construct their own organizers.

Examples of Visual Representations: **Semantic Maps**

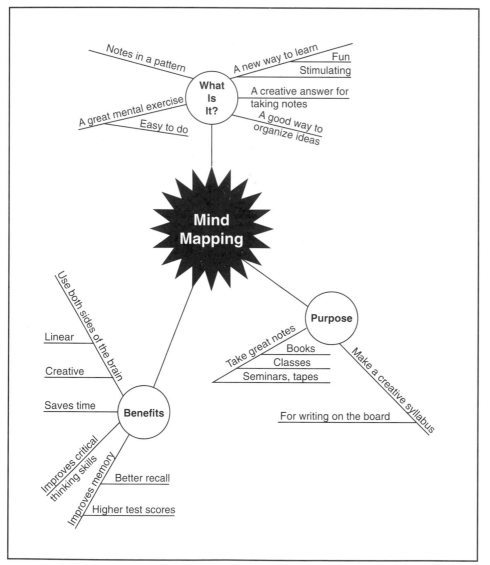

Note: From *Semantic mapping: classroom applications* by Joan E. Heimlich and Susan D. Pittleman, 1986, Newark, DE: International Reading Association. Copyright © 1986 by International Reading Association. Reprinted with permission.

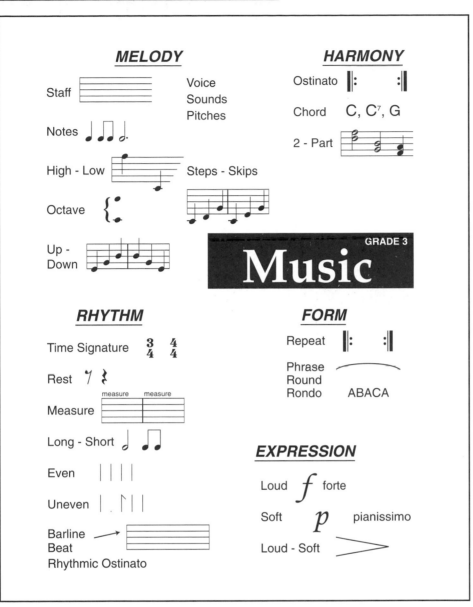

Note: **From** *Semantic mapping: classroom applications* **by Joan E. Heimlich and Susan D. Pittleman, 1986, Newark, DE: International Reading Association. Copyright © 1986 by International Reading Association. Reprinted with permission.**

Informational Text

19. Group Summarizing

What is it?

Class summaries help learners review and remember information. Summarizing information requires that readers distinguish between key concepts and subordinate ideas. It also requires the ability to condense information (Brown, Day & Jones, 1983). Summarizing is a sophisticated skill; therefore, modeling this skill is critical.

How to use it:

1. Have students survey the text passage to identify major topics on which to focus while reading. For example, if the reading is to be about armadillos and the sub-headings in the text are "description," "food," "homes," and "interesting facts," these subheadings will become the areas students will use in their summaries.

2. Next, divide the chalkboard or chart paper into four parts and label the sections "Description," "Food," "Homes," and "Interesting Facts." These sections provide the students with a purpose for reading.

3. After the students have read the text, ask the class to volunteer information for each of the categories on the chalkboard. Record the information in sentence form. Class discussion is a key part of the process. Students need to understand which concepts are most important and how they can be stated clearly.

4. Class summaries are then developed from the recorded information. The summaries are written on each part of the chart for students to read.

Informational Text

Examples of Visual Representations: **Group Summary**

Sample Organizational Format for Group Summarizing Activity	
Description Nine-banded armadillos are about two feet long and weigh about fifteen pounds. They have strong claws for digging and a shell of hard, bony plates for protection.	**Food** Armadillos eat insects, earthworms, spiders, and landsnails by licking them up.
Home Armadillos live in a tunnel hole filled with leaves to keep them warm.	**Interesting Facts** Armadillos protect themselves by digging a hole or curling into a ball. They have four babies at a time that are all males or all females.

Note: From "Content reading instruction in the primary grades: perceptions and strategies," by M.W. Olson and T.C. Gee, 1991, in *The Reading Teacher, 45* (4). Copyright © 1991 by the International Reading Association. Reprinted with permission.

Informational Text

20. Informational Paragraph Frames

What is it?

When children retell what they have read, comprehension is improved. Expository paragraph frames are tools children can use to practice retelling. They can also be used to review and reinforce specific content and to help students see different ways authors organize material in order to inform.

How to use it:

1. Create a paragraph frame that corresponds to the organization of details in the content passage to be read.

2. Assign the reading selection and then ask for volunteers to retell what they read.

3. Present the paragraph frame to students and ask them to fill in the missing information. Encourage students to discuss information not mentioned in the frame.

The skills and habits children acquire with primary-level content texts will help them as the number and diversity of textbooks increase in later grades.

Informational Text

Examples of Visual Representations: **Informational Paragraph Frames**

Process frame (Based on a passage about how cloth is made.)

Making cloth is an interesting process.

The first part of the process is _____

_____

The next step in the process is_____

_____

The third step in the process is _____

_____

It is interesting to learn how cloth is made.

Contrast frame (Based on a passage comparing oceans and lakes.)

Oceans and lakes are different in several ways. They are different in size. Oceans are _____ than lakes. Their water is different, too. Ocean water is _____ while lake water is _____. Different kinds of fish live in oceans and lakes. _____ and _____ fish live only in ocean water while _____ and _____ fish live only in lakes. It is interesting to learn how oceans and lakes are different.

Note: **Adapted from "Content reading instruction in the primary grades: perceptions and strategies," by M.W. Olson and T.C. Gee, 1991, in *The Reading Teacher*, 45 (4). Copyright © 1991 by the International Reading Association. Used with permission.**

Informational Text Frame example

From the title and subtitles of this selection (chapter), I believe that the major points will be _____ .
Examples that will be used to illustrate each point will be _____ , _____ , and _____ .

Note: **From "Content reading instruction in the primary grades: perceptions and strategies," by M.W. Olson and T.C. Gee, 1991, in *The Reading Teacher*, 45 (4). Copyright © 1991 by the International Reading Association. Reprinted with permission.**

Informational Text

21. What I Know; Want to Learn; Learned (K-W-L)

What is it?

Another strategy that helps children predict and connect new information with prior knowledge is K-W-L (Ogle, 1986, 1989). K-W-L can be used in class to brainstorm prior knowledge, to preview vocabulary and concepts, and to help students recall what they have read. The strategy also focuses students on assigned text and allows the teacher to model what effective readers do with reading assignments in the content areas.

How to use it:

1. The teacher draws three columns on the board or chart paper. These chart paper examples can be kept and referred to throughout the reading. If students complete the task individually, they can use a prepared form with the three column labels, or they can make their own.

2. During the first phase of the strategy, students brainstorm about what they *Know*, or think they know, about the main topic. For example, before reading a chapter describing toads, students would list the facts they already know about this topic in the *Know* column. As the teacher records the children's contributions, he shows how to organize the ideas into categories.

3. Next, students list what they *Want* to know about the topic. Students list interesting questions that come to mind as a result of identifying what they think they know. For the topic of toads, students might ask: How long do toads live and what do they contribute to nature? What exactly is the process? How do toads protect themselves?

4. Students then read the chapter purposefully because they want to discover answers for the questions they have posed. The last step in the K-W-L process is for students to identify what they have *Learned*. Here, students record the answers to their questions as well as any other important information they have

Informational Text

learned. Sometimes students find out that what they thought they knew was inaccurate.

5. A variation of K-W-L is K-W-L-W-H. After students complete the L column, they record *What* else they want to learn about the topic and *How* they will find that information. Using this variation reinforces that learning does not end when class ends, but is a lifelong process.

Examples of Visual Representations: **K-W-L Worksheets**

K What I know	W What I want to find out	L What I learned

Note: From "Content reading instruction in the primary grades: perceptions and strategies," by M.W. Olson and T.C. Gee, 1991, in *The Reading Teacher*, 45 (4). Copyright © 1991 by the International Reading Association. Reprinted with permission.

K-W-L Worksheet for a Science Selection on Toads

K What we know	W What we want to find out	L What we learned and still need to learn
1 small animal 1 gray 1 has a long tongue 3 jumps 3 spits poison 2 eats bugs 2 eats spiders **Categories** 1. description 2. food 3. what toads do	Are toads the same as frogs? If not, how are they different? Where do toads live in the winter? in the summer? How do toads protect themselves? How far can they jump?	

Note: From "Content reading instruction in the primary grades: perceptions and strategies," by M.W. Olson and T.C. Gee, 1991, in *The Reading Teacher, 45* (4). Copyright © 1991 by the International Reading Association. Reprinted with permission.

Informational Text

22. Pairs Read

What is it?

Pairs Read is a strategy that requires collaborative learning as students read and digest text. Students help each other increase their knowledge and understanding of the text by reading the text aloud to each other. While one student reads aloud, the other student listens and then summarizes what she heard as the main ideas.

How to use it:

Option 1

1. Select a passage for the students to read.

2. Arrange students into pairs with one being the coach and the other being the reader.

3. The reader reads the first paragraph of the selected passage out loud to the coach.

4. After reading, the coach summarizes the main idea of the paragraph and discusses any supporting details necessary for understanding. The coach can ask the reader questions to help clarify the reading.

5. The students reverse roles, and the new reader reads the next paragraph to the coach.

6. The new coach summarizes the main idea of the paragraph and discusses any supporting details necessary for understanding.

7. Students continue alternating roles to read and summarize as they complete the passage.

8. Once the entire passage is read, the students cooperatively summarize the main idea and discuss the supporting details.

Option 2

1. Select a passage for the students to read.

2. Arrange students into pairs with one being the reader and one being the coach.

3. Students read the first paragraph, half of the passage, or the entire passage silently (the more difficult the material, the greater the need to break the reading of the passage into smaller chunks for understanding).

4. After reading, the reader summarizes the passage for the coach. The role of the coach is to ask effective, probing, and clarifying questions.

5. Students reverse roles, read the next section silently, and the reader then summarizes for the coach with the coach asking questions.

6. The process continues until the entire passage has been read and summarized.

7. Once the entire passage is read, the students cooperatively summarize the main idea of the passage and discuss the supporting details.

Informational Text

23. Prereading Plan (PreP)

What is it?

The Prereading Plan (PreP) (Langer, 1981) provides a framework for activating and extending prior knowledge.

How to use it.

1. Identify the central concept in the selection and introduce it to the students by saying, "What comes to your mind when you hear the word (or phrase) _____ ? (e.g., "Internet")

2. Individually, have students write all of their associations, and then on the chalkboard make a composite list of all of the different responses (e.g. "technology," "World Wide Web," "search," "e-mail").

3. Have students reflect on why each association was made by asking, "What made you think of _____ ? (e.g. "I use e-mail to communicate with our cousins in Mexico.")

4. Conclude the activity by saying, "As a result of our discussion, can you think of any other information that you know about this topic?" (e.g., "Just because something is printed on the Internet doesn't mean it's a fact.)

Informational Text

24. Problematic Situations

What is it?

Problematic Situations is a strategy that activates what students already know about the topic, motivates students to want to read the text, and helps them to focus on the main ideas presented in the text as they read. Developed by Vacca and Vacca (1993), it can be used with any text material that deals with a problem/solution relationship.

How to use it:

1. Design a problematic situation similar to the one presented in the text passage. Provide enough relevant information about the situation so students will be able to focus their attention on the key ideas in the passage they will read. Be sure to clearly define the context of the problem.

   Social studies students learning about the Cuban missile crisis might be presented with following dilemma:

   > You are President of the United States and have just been informed by the CIA that your archenemy has been installing offensive nuclear warheads in a small country sixty miles away from the U.S. Based on your knowledge of the Cold War, what steps would you take in this situation?

2. Pose the problem to the students and in cooperative groups have them generate possible results or solutions. Each group should record their responses. When they have listed their solutions, have them discuss why each one is a good solution, or would succeed.

   High school students might be presented with the following scenario for an interdisciplinary unit in math and consumer science:

   > Your firm has been selected to design a new package for the STARBAR Candy Company. The company is planning to reduce the size of the original bar by 10 percent.

The dimensions of the current bar are:

length: 6 inches   width: 2 inches   depth: 1 inch

The company must reduce the size to cut costs, but they recognize that reducing the size may affect sales. Your task is to design the packaging so that it will minimize the appearance of the reduction in size. Write your response in the form of a proposal to the chairman of the board for STARBAR Candy. Proposals are due on

_____ .

3. Students "test" their solutions when they read the assigned text material. Have each group refine or modify their solutions as they gain new information from their reading.

4. As a final activity, discuss with the class whether some of the students' solutions might be better than that presented by the author.

Informational Text

25. Proposition/Support Outlines

What is it?

Proposition/Support Outlines (Buehl, 1995) help students learn to be critical readers who can recognize different viewpoints, theories, hypotheses, and debatable assertions made by authors. In addition, Proposition/Support Outlines offer students a framework for analyzing the different types of evidence an author presents to support his proposition.

How to use it:

1. Initiate a discussion of the difference between facts and opinions by brainstorming with students a definition of each and then generating a list of examples for each. "The Colorado Rockies home field is named Coors Field" is a fact statement, while "The Colorado Rockies is a great baseball team" is an opinion that may or may not be supported by facts.

2. Introduce the term "proposition"– a statement that can be argued as true. Provide students with several possible propositions; for example, Nebraska is America's corn state; today's movies are too violent; the school playground needs new playground equipment; or gun control prevents crime. Divide students into cooperative groups and assign each group the task of generating as many arguments as they can that might be used to support one of these propositions.

3. In large group sharing, help students categorize the types of arguments that could be used to support a proposition. Introduce, for example, a blank Proposition/Support Outline on an overhead transparency, and model for students how support for a proposition could be categorized as facts, statistics, examples, expert authority, logic, or reasoning.

4. Assign a text passage that follows a Proposition/Support frame of writing and have students complete the Proposition/Support Outline as they analyze the author's arguments. (Select for student practice a text that features a

clear proposition.) Initially, it may be desirable to have students work in pairs to (1) identify the proposition, and (2) share how they used the clues in the text to identify it.

Students then use the outline to categorize the arguments supporting the proposition. For example, an article on rain forests might contain information and arguments that are reflected in all five support categories.

5. Analyze with students the type of support presented.

6. As students become confident using Proposition/Support Outlines, they may be asked to use them in a variety of contexts, such as in an investigation of different propositions possible from a textbook passage. For example, some students may read a passage on the Vietnam War to locate support for the proposition: "The U.S. did the right thing by sending troops to Vietnam." Other students may be asked to support the proposition: "The U.S. should not have entered the Vietnam war."

The Proposition/Support Outline is an excellent guide for independent research. It provides students with a framework for examining reference material for relevant information and arguments.

Examples of Visual Representations: **Proposition/Support Outlines**

Proposition/Support

Topic: Rain Forests

Proposition: The loss of our rain forests will lead to an environmental disaster.

Support:

1. Facts
- Rain forests use up carbon dioxide.
- There is increased carbon dioxide in the earth's atmosphere.
- The rain forests contain many endangered plant and animal species.
- Deforestation leads to widespread soil erosion in many areas.
- The burning of fossil fuels puts carbon dioxide into the environment.

2. Statistics
- The 1980s were the "hottest" decade in the last 100 years.
- One acre of tropical forest disappears every second.
- 4 million acres (larger than the state of Connecticut) disappear every year.
- 50 to 100 species are destroyed with each acre of rain forest cleared.
- If present trends continue, half of the rain forests of Honduras and Nicaragua will disappear by the year 2000.

3. Examples
- India has almost no remaining rain forest.
- Current plans target eliminating of much of the Congo's rain forest.
- Run-off from deforestation in Indonesia threatens their coral reefs and diminishes the fish population.
- Cutting of rain forests in Bangladesh and the Phillipines has led to killer floods.

4. Expert Authority
- Computers predict doubling of carbon dioxide in the next century, raising temperatures 3 to 9 degrees.
- National Center for Atmospheric Research believes increased carbon dioxide will lead to Greenhouse Effect and global warming.
- Environmentalist expert Al Gore calls Greenhouse Effect our most serious threat ever.

5. Logic and Reasoning
- Warmer temperatures will harm crops and increase energy costs.
- More people will starve because of less food and increased population growth.
- The polar glaciers will melt and raise the sea level, flooding coastlines.
- Many species useful to humans will disappear.
- More sections of the world will become uninhabitable deserts due to soil loss from erosion, overgrazing, and overcultivation.

Note: From *Classroom strategies for interactive learning,* by Doug Buehl, 1995, Schofield, WI: Wisconsin State Reading Association. Copyright © 1995 by the Wisconsin State Reading Association. Reprinted with permission.

Proposition/Support

Topic:

Proposition:

Support:

1. Facts

2. Statistics

3. Examples

4. Expert Authority

5. Logic and Reasoning

Note: From *Classroom strategies for interactive learning,* by Doug Buehl, 1995, Schofield, WI: Wisconsin State Reading Association. Copyright © 1995 by the Wisconsin State Reading Association. Reprinted with permission.

Informational Text

26. Reciprocal Teaching

What is it?

Reciprocal Teaching (Palincsar & Brown, 1985) is a strategy in which students learn the skills of summarizing, questioning, clarifying and predicting well enough to perform as an instructor of content. When students become adept at these four skills, they not only instruct one another but also learn metacomprehension skills they can use while reading independently.

How to use it:

1. Explain to students the concept of reciprocal teaching—that we learn best what we have to teach others.

2. Identify each of the four skills or strategies students will learn in order to help their classmates comprehend and remember what they read. Point out that learning these skills will also help improve students' own reading comprehension. These skills are

   - Summarizing: identifying and condensing the most important points in the text.

   - Questioning: formulating questions about what you don't know, what you need to know, or what you would like to know concerning the subject of a text passage.

   - Clarifying: making sense of confusing text and potential barriers to comprehension, such as new vocabulary terms, unclear referents, difficult concepts.

   - Predicting: using information already given in the text, text structure, graphic aids, and background knowledge to formulate a guess about where the text "is going."

3. Model for students how to summarize, generate questions, clarify confusing text, and predict. Then, give students one day of practice for each of these skills. For instance, students can practice the skill of summarizing by recounting highlights from a book, movie or television show. Next, they can practice this

skill by identifying the main idea in different textbook paragraphs and then in longer passages.

4. After students have practiced each of these skills, begin to shift some of the responsibility for directing discussion onto the students. Call on each member of the class to participate at some level. Provide guidance and feedback to students. For instance, you might prompt the student teacher by asking, "What question do you think a teacher would ask at this point?" Or suggest that a student teacher who is struggling with question-generating try to summarize the passage first. Soliciting help from the other students can also take the focus off of you as the teacher and keep the students in control of the dialogue.

5. As students become more proficient, assign a longer passage. Model the entire process one more time, explaining at each stage why you are using each skill. Then, assign another text passage and have students take turns being student teacher for small groups.

Informational Text

27. SQ3R (Survey, Question, Read, Recite, Review)

What is it?

SQ3R (Robinson, 1961) is a versatile study strategy because it engages students during each phase of the reading process. Students preview the text material to develop predictions and to set a purpose for reading by generating questions about the topic; they read actively, searching for answers to those questions; they monitor their comprehension as they summarize; and they evaluate their comprehension through review activities.

How to use it:

Provide students with a copy of the following instructions. Model how you would respond to each set of questions or tasks. Assign a text passage to be read and have students practice the strategy in pairs or small groups. When it's clear that they understand each phase of the strategy, assign additional passages to be read, but have students work individually on the strategy.

1. Survey what you are about to read.

   - Think about the title: What do I know about this subject? What do I want to know?

   - Glance over headings and/or skim the first sentences of paragraphs.

   - Look at illustrations and graphic aids.

   - Read the first paragraph.

   - Read the last paragraph or summary.

2. Question.

   - Turn the title into a question. This becomes the major purpose for your reading.

   - Write down any questions that come to mind during the survey.

Informational Text

- Turn headings into questions.

- Turn subheadings, illustrations, and graphic aids into questions.

- Write down unfamiliar vocabulary and determine the meaning.

3. Read actively.

- Read to search for answers to questions.

- Respond to questions and use context clues for unfamiliar words.

- React to unclear passages, confusing terms, and questionable statements by generating additional questions.

4. Recite.

- Look away from the answers and the book to recall what was read.

- Recite answers to questions aloud or in writing.

- Reread text for unanswered questions.

5. Review.

- Answer the major purpose questions.

- Look over answers and all parts of the chapter to organize information.

- Summarize the information learned by creating a graphic organizer that depicts the main ideas, by drawing a flow chart, by writing a summary, by participating in a group discussion, or by writing an explanation of how this material has changed your perceptions or applies to your life.

Informational Text

28. Search Strategy

What is it?

The Search Strategy is used when students are asked to research a topic. The project should focus on a question to be answered rather than on a general topic. This comprehensive strategy will stimulate students to find answers to questions they have generated from their reading.

How to use it:

1. Select a specific topic of interest to study.

2. Establish what students know, think they know, and want to know about the topic. Write the three categories on chart paper or the chalkboard. Have them work individually first, then in small groups to stimulate ideas. Record ideas in all three categories. Encourage participation from all students and develop confidence by suggesting they know more than they realize.

3. Ask questions to raise curiosity and to challenge students by asking for more specific information when they share their ideas about the topic.

4. Read resource material to verify what they know and think they know, to answer questions, and to raise new questions.

5. Come together like scholars; share and review responses in small groups.

6. Have a large group discussion to share learnings, and to identify unanswered as well as new questions for further research.

Examples of Visual Representations: **Search Strategy**

Search Strategy

S	
E	
A	
R	
C	
H	

Adapted from Harvey Silver - Silver and Strong Associates, Inc.

Informational Text

29. Semantic Mapping

What is it?

Semantic Mapping (Johnson & Pearson, 1984) can be used as both a prereading and post reading strategy. Its purpose is to depict the relationships among key concepts and related technical terms in a text passage. As such, it works well as an introduction to a topic and vocabulary students may encounter during reading. It can be used as a review strategy in which students not only map key concepts but also indicate hierarchies that exist among concepts and related technical terms. To use as a prereading strategy:

How to use it:

1. Model for students how to perform the strategy:

   Write on the board a key concept from the unit you have just completed.

   List a number of related concepts and technical terms. (These may come from the text or simply be part of your general knowledge base about the topic.) As you create this list, explain your thought process: why the key concept made you think of each term you listed, and the connections you see between each term and the key concept. Next, create a web or map for the terms you have listed. In order to do that, you will need to classify, or group, these terms into categories. Verbalize your thoughts as you identify appropriate categories, label each, and write the terms under the appropriate category label.

2. When students understand the semantic mapping strategy, write on the board a key concept from the lesson you are about to teach. Have students collaborate in small groups to brainstorm as many related words and concepts as they can think of. Ask them to help the recorder classify the words into groups.

McREL

Informational Text

3. The semantic maps created by the small groups are then shared to create one large semantic map on the board. Add any missing words that students will need to know to understand the passage.

4. After students finish reading the text passage, ask them to add new information they learned. Using a different color chalk will highlight which terms are a product of new learning.

Examples of Visual Representation: **Semantic Map**

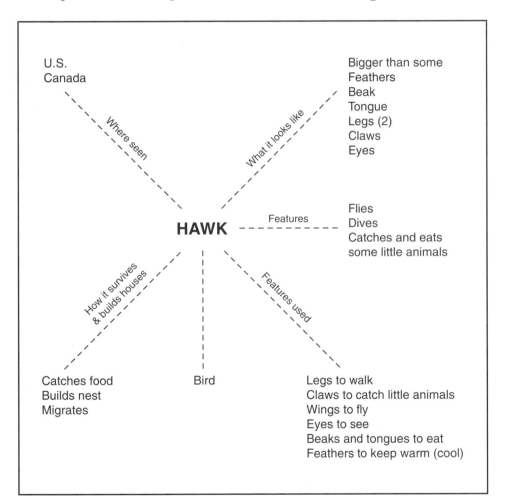

Note: **From "Content reading instruction in the primary grades: perceptions and strategies," by M.W. Olson and T.C. Gee, 1991, in** *The Reading Teacher,* **45 (4). Copyright © 1991 by the International Reading Association. Reprinted with permission.**

Informational Text

30. Sensory Imagery

What is it?

Comprehension, recall, and retention can be enhanced through sensory imaging while reading.

Imagining what something looks like, smells like, feels like, even tastes like can become a hook to connect new information to prior knowledge. Many younger children are adept at imaging, judging from their fantasy play. Transferring this skill to content area reading can stimulate interest in reading and learning.

How to use it:

1. Select a text passage that contains sensory details (e.g., a sheep shearing).

2. As students follow along in their texts, read the passage aloud. At appropriate points, stop and ask students to imagine the scene: "The text describes a farmer shearing his sheep. Have you ever seen a sheep up close, maybe on a farm or on TV? What did its coat look like? What color was it?" Allow some time for students to share their experiences. Continue to prompt them to visualize the scene. "What does the book say about how the sheep behaves during the shearing?"; "What sounds do you think they'd make?"; "Has anyone here ever smelled a farm that has sheep? Can you describe that smell? Just thinking of it makes my nose wrinkle!"

3. Select another vivid passage for the class to read aloud. This time have students volunteer their images.

4. Ask students what they discovered about using their imagination while reading. Periodically revisit this strategy to reinforce its use during independent reading.

Informational Text

31. Structured Note-taking

What is it?

As the name implies, Structured Note-taking (Smith & Tompkins, 1988) helps students take notes more effectively. Over 50 percent of the material that students read or hear in class is forgotten in a matter of minutes (Vacca & Vacca, 1993). Therefore, using a note-taking system that assists in recall and retention of information is essential. Structured Note-taking is one of a variety of note-taking strategies; however, it offers students a visual framework that can help them determine just which information to include as they take notes. Initially, the teacher provides students with a graphic organizer that mimics the organizational pattern in the text to be read. Eventually, as students practice this skill, they learn to devise their own graphic organizers.

How to use it:

1. Instruct students in the various organizational patterns authors use. Seven of these were described earlier in the manual. Explain that understanding these patterns improves understanding of the text and also provides a structure for taking notes on the material.

2. Once students understand the different organizational patterns, model structured note-taking. Give students a short passage for which you have already created a graphic organizer and walk them through how you would use it for note-taking.

3. Next, assign a passage from the text from which students can take notes. Provide each student with a copy of a graphic organizer you have constructed for that passage. You may want to include major headings on the organizer, so that students can be successful at ordering subordinate ideas on the graphic. Point out that at first you will be giving them prepared organizers, but that eventually they will be able to build their own as they read. After they have finished reading

and note-taking, students can share their work with a partner, explaining why they included certain information and justifying its position on the graphic.

4. Continue to scaffold student learning over time, constructing graphics for students but leaving all of the boxes or circles empty for them to fill in. Then, show students how to preview text as the basis for constructing an accurate visual representation of the material.

5. As students develop confidence with Structured Note-taking, they will begin to develop their own visual frameworks.

Examples of Visual Representations: **Structured Note-taking**

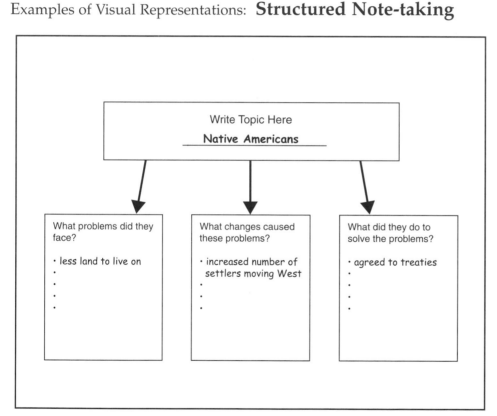

Note: **From "Structured notetaking: a new strategy for content area readers." by P. Smith and G. Tompkins, 1988, in** *Journal of Reading,* **32(1), pp. 46-53. Copyright © 1988 by the International Reading Association. Reprinted with permission.**

Informational Text

32. "Think-alouds"

What is it?

"Think-alouds" (Davey, 1983) help students understand the kind of thinking required by a specific task. The teacher models her thinking process by verbalizing her thoughts as she reads, processes information, or performs some learning task. Students see how the teacher attempts to construct meaning for unfamiliar vocabulary, engages in dialogue with the author, or recognizes when she isn't comprehending and selects a fix-up strategy that addresses a problem she is having. Ineffective readers especially benefit from observing what skilled readers think about while reading.

How to use it:

1. Explain that reading is a complex process that involves thinking and sense-making; the skilled reader's mind is alive with questions she asks herself in order to understand what she reads.

2. Select a passage to read aloud that contains points that students might find difficult, unknown vocabulary terms, or ambiguous wording. Develop questions you can ask yourself that will show what you think as you confront these problems while reading.

3. While students read this passage silently, read it aloud. As you read, verbalize your thoughts, the questions you develop, and the process you use to solve comprehension problems. It is helpful if you alter the tone of your voice, so students know when you are reading and at what points you begin and end thinking aloud.

4. Coping strategies you can model include

   - making predictions or hypotheses as you read: "From what he's said so far, I'll bet that the author is going to give some examples of poor eating habits."

- describing the mental pictures you "see": "When the author talks about vegetables I should include in my diet, I can see our salad bowl at home filled with fresh, green spinach leaves."

- demonstrating how you connect this information with prior knowledge: "'Saturated fat'? I know I've heard that term before. I learned it last year when we studied nutrition."

- creating analogies: "That description of clogged arteries sounds like traffic clogging up the interstate during rush hour."

- verbalizing obstacles and fix-up strategies: "Now what does 'angiogram' mean? Maybe if I reread that section, I'll get the meaning from the other sentences around it. I know I can't skip it because it's in bold-faced print, so it must be important. If I still don't understand, I know I can ask the teacher for help."

5. Have students work with partners to practice "think-alouds" when reading short passages of text. Periodically revisit this strategy or have students complete the assessment that follows so these metacomprehension skills become second nature.

Examples of Visual Representations: **"Think-aloud" Assessment**

Assessing My Use of the "Think-aloud" Strategy

While I was reading, how much did I use these "think-aloud" strategies?

	Not much	A little	Most of the time	All of the time
Making and revising predictions				
Forming mental pictures				
Connecting what I read to what I already know				
Creating analogies				
Verbalizing confusing points				
Using fix-up strategies				

Reflection Strategies

33. Concept Question Chain

What is it?

The Concept Question Chain (Johnson, 1992) is similar to QAR in that both require students to use higher order thinking skills when they formulate responses to questions about what they have read. As such, it is a valuable tool for in-class and independent reading. The Concept Question Chain consists of three levels of questioning: literal, interpretive, and applied. All questions are designed to help students grasp the meaning of the text-based concept or theme and to apply it to another situation.

How to use it:

1. Select one important concept or theme from the text about which you want students to have a thorough understanding.

2. Construct questions about this concept at each of the following three levels:

   - "Right There" or literal questions; the reader can literally put her finger on the answer in the text. Questions begin with phrases such as "who is," "where is," "list," "what is," "when is," "how many," "when did," "name," and "what kind of." There is one right answer to the question, and it can be stated in just a few words.

   - "Think and Search" or interpretive questions; the reader makes inferences and discerns relationships about the author's ideas. The answers are found in the text, but may require that the reader connect ideas located in different parts of the text. Questions begin with words such as "summarize," "contrast," "explain," "find two examples," "why did," "how did," and "what caused."

   - "On My Own" or applied questions; the reader is expected to evaluate text-based information, or apply it to a different situation or context. The answers to these questions are found beyond the text in conjunction with the reader's prior knowledge. Questions begin with phrases such as "what do you think about," "prove," "apply," "what if," "what would you do if," "evaluate," "how would this be different if" and "suggest."

Begin by designing questions for the interpretive level, as this level provides direction for developing the appropriate literal and applied questions; the latter should encourage students to think about the text-based concept in a broader perspective and to apply the concept beyond the text selection. Write questions that will cause the students to connect ideas and interpret important information so they understand the concept. When developing questions, remember that quantity is not as important as the "thoughtfulness" of each question.

3. After preparing students for reading (i.e., activating background knowledge, introducing key vocabulary, and identifying the purpose for reading), assign the reading selection and tell students to focus on the concept as they read. Provide them with a question from each level to guide their reading and to show them that you want them to read at more than the literal level alone.

4. Encourage structured note-taking that addresses the questions you have posed.

5. After the students have read the selection, lead a discussion using the questions you have developed. Then, have students demonstrate their understanding of the concept by completing a performance task. For example, instruct students to

- Develop a short script for a radio news broadcast that illustrates the concept in today's news.

- Write a poem about the concept.

- Select a song that you feel illustrates the concept. Share it with the class, explaining why it represents the concept for you.

Reflection Strategies

- Create a visual that depicts the concept. Be prepared to explain how it illustrates what the concept means to you.

- Write an editorial expressing your views on how the concept is important to today's society.

Adapted from Barbara E. Johnson, 1992

Reflection Strategies

34. Question-Answer Relationships (QAR)

What is it?

QAR (Raphael, 1982; 1986) is a strategy that is "designed to demystify the questioning process, providing teachers and students with a common vocabulary to discuss different types of questions and sources of information for answering these questions...." (Anthony & Raphael, p. 319). Four levels of questions are studied during strategy use and practice. Two are text-based QARs:

- "Right There" questions ask students to respond at the literal level; the words used to formulate the question and used to answer the question can be found "right there" in the same sentence of the text. "Right There" questions begin with words or statements such as "who is," "where is," "list," "what is," "when is," "how many," "when did," "name," "what kind of." These questions usually elicit a one-word or short-phrase response and require one right answer. Sample questions are "Who discovered America?" or "Who was the first person to walk on the moon?"

- "Think and Search" questions require students to "think" about how the information or ideas in the text relate to one another, and to "search" through the entire passage they read to find information that applies. "Think and Search" questions may begin with words or statements such as "summarize," "what caused," "contrast," "retell," "how did," "explain," "find two examples," "for what reason," or "compare." A sample question is, "Which strategies could the individual described in this chapter use to improve his financial situation?"

The other QARs could be called knowledge-based because students must use their prior knowledge to answer the question:

- "Author and You" questions require students to answer with information not in the text; however, students must have read the text material to understand what the question is asking. A sample question is, "The topic of the passage was cloning. In what instances, if ever, do you think cloning should be used?"

- "On My Own" questions can be answered with information from the students' background knowledge and do not require reading the text.

Students who become skilled at this strategy recognize the relationship between the questions teachers ask and the answers they expect; therefore, they know where to find information needed for a correct response. Although teaching this strategy can take time, Richardson and Morgan (1994) report that students who learned and practiced this strategy for as little as eight weeks showed significant gains in reading comprehension.

Anthony and Raphael assert that QAR can also facilitate the transfer of control of the questioning process from teacher to learner. That is, when students become skilled at QAR, they need to rely less on their teacher because they are able to generate different levels of questions, themselves, during independent reading.

How to use it:

1. Introduce the strategy by giving students a written and verbal description of each question-answer relationship.

2. Assign short passages to be read from the textbook. As students finish reading each passage, ask them one question from each QAR category. Point out the differences between each question and the kind of answer it requires.

3. After students demonstrate that they understand the differences among the four QAR levels, assign several more short passages to be read. Again, ask one question for each category of QAR per passage, provide students with answers to the questions, and identify each question's QAR type. Discuss why the questions represent one QAR but not another.

4. Next, assign short text passages, and provide the questions and the answers. This time, however, have students identify each question as a particular QAR and explain their answer. Repeat the reading and questioning process, but have students work in groups to determine which QAR each question represents and write out their answers, accordingly.

5. At this point have students read a longer text passage. Give them several questions, not necessarily one per QAR level. Have students individually determine the QAR and write their answers. Continue assigning longer passages and various QARs for students to identify and answer.

6. Eventually, when reading is assigned in class, students should generate various QARs on their own that they present to the rest of the class for identification and answers.

Reflection Strategies

35. Learning Logs

What is it?

One of the most effective means of writing-to-learn is keeping a learning log. Learning logs foster reflection on either text content or on students' reading and learning processes. Learning logs differ from journals in that they focus on content covered in class, not students' personal and private feelings. Students may reflect on how they feel, but it is always in relation to what is being studied in class.

How to use it:

1. Select the concept or process you want students to explore.

2. A learning log entry can be assigned at any time during class, depending upon the topic and your purpose. For example, you would assign the following topic in the middle of a reading assignment in class: Based upon what you have read thus far, explain whether your initial predictions about the story/ passage were correct.

3. Assign the topic, and give students three to five minutes "think time" to consider their response.

4. Have students write for five minutes on the learning log topic.

5. You might have students reread their learning log entries at a later date and reflect on how their ideas have changed.

Possible learning log topics:

- Explain which prereading strategy we learned has made the most difference in your reading comprehension, and why.

- Which "fix-up" strategies do you use most often when you read? Explain how they have helped your comprehension.

- Advise a younger brother, sister, or friend on ways to stay focused when reading at home.

- Which of the textbooks you are using this year is the most difficult for you to understand? Analyze what it is about that particular text that makes it hard to comprehend.

- Which story or text passage we read during this unit have you found the most interesting? Explain your answer.

- One topic we have studied during this unit is _____. Why do you think this topic has been included as part of this course?

- Write about the importance of _____ (an idea or concept students have read about) to the world in general, and to you in particular.

- Write about an idea or concept in the text that confuses you. What is it that you find particularly hard to understand? What could you do to gain a better understanding of this idea or concept?

- Summarize the text material we read in class today. Explain how it relates to or reminds you of information or skills you have learned elsewhere.

- Write a letter to the editor of the school paper in which you argue for or against a controversial issue we are studying or have studied this year.

- Write about an upcoming test or quiz. List the questions that you think might be asked, and develop answers for each.

- Consider how your opinions have changed as a result of what we have studied during this unit. How have class discussion, reading, or class activities influenced the way you think about the topic of the unit?

- Discuss what we have been reading with a specific audience— a teenager from another time period, a young child, a new student.

Reflection Strategies

- Write a 30-second ad for station _____ (the radio station you listen to most) in which you "sell" the listeners on the benefits of learning about an idea we have studied during this unit.

Reflection Strategies

36. RAFT—Role/Audience/Format/Topic

The RAFT strategy (Santa, 1988) employs writing-to-learn activities to enhance understanding of informational text. Instead of writing a traditional essay explaining a concept learned, students demonstrate their understanding in a nontraditional format. This technique encourages creative thinking and motivates students to reflect in unusual ways about concepts they have read.

RAFT is an acronym that stands for

- **Role** of the writer. What is the writer's role: reporter, observer, eyewitness?

- **Audience.** Who will be reading this writing: the teacher, other students, a parent, people in the community, an editor?

- **Format.** What is the best way to present this writing: in a letter, an article, a report, a poem?

- **Topic.** Who or what is the subject of this writing: a famous mathematician, a prehistoric cave dweller, a reaction to a specific event?

The RAFT strategy forces students to process information, rather than merely write out answers to questions. Students are more motivated to undertake the writing assignment because it involves them personally and allows for more creative responses to learning the material.

How to use it:

1. Analyze the important ideas or information that you want students to learn from reading a story, a textbook passage, or other material. Consider how writing might enhance students' understanding of the topic (e.g, stages of the digestive system, or the frustrations of slaves before and after the Civil War). This focus establishes the topic for writing.

2. Brainstorm possible roles students could assume in their writing. For example, a student in an automotive class could imagine he was a spark plug and describe what occurs when an engine starts. A student studying America's involvement in Vietnam could assume the role of a farmer whose land becomes the site of a battle.

3. Next, decide who the audience will be for this communication and determine the format for the writing. For example, the spark plug could be writing in the format of a diary to be read by other spark plugs just placed in new cars. The Vietnamese farmer could be writing in the form of a petition for the war to end.

4. After students have finished reading, explain RAFT and list the role, audience, format, and topic for the writing. All students could be assigned the same role for their writing, or you could offer several different roles from which students can choose.

Reflection Strategies

Examples of Visual Representation: **RAFT**

Examples of RAFT Assignments

Role	Audience	Format	Topic
Newspaper Reporter	Readers in the 1870s	Obituary	Qualities of General Custer
Lawyer	U.S. Supreme Court	Appeal Speech	Dred Scott Decision
Abraham Lincoln	Dear Abby	Advice Column	Problems with his generals
Mike Royko	Public	News Column	Capital punishment
Frontier Woman	Self	Diary	Hardships in the West
Constituent	U.S. Senator	Letter	Gun Control
Newswriter	Public	News Release	Ozone layer has been formed
Chemist	Chemical company	Instructions	Combinations to avoid
Wheat Thin	Other Wheat Thins	Travel Guide	Journey through the digestive system
Plant	Sun	Thank-you note	Sun's role in plant's growth
Scientist	Charles Darwin	Letter	Refute a point in evolution theory
Square Root	Whole Number	Love letter	Explain relationship
Repeating Decimal	Set of Rational Numbers	Petition	Prove you belong to this set
Cook	Other Cooks	Recipe	Alcoholism
Julia Child	TV Audience	Script	Wonders of eggs
Advertiser	TV Audience	Public Service	Importance of fruit
Lungs	Cigarettes	Complaint	Effects of smoking
Huck Finn	Jim	Letter	What I learned during the trip
Joseph Stalin	George Orwell	Letter	Reactions to *Animal Farm*
Comma	9th grade students	Complaint	How it is misused
Trout	Self	Diary	Effects of acid rain on lake

Note: **From *Classroom strategies for interactive learning,* by Doug Buehl, 1995, Schofield, WI: Wisconsin State Reading Association. Copyright © 1995 by the Wisconsin State Reading Association. Reprinted with permission.**

Reflection Strategies

37. Writing-to-Learn

What is it?

Writing to learn is a method "that can (and should) be incorporated across the curriculum. This approach helps students personalize learning so that they understand their course work better and retain what they have learned longer. It also encourages high-level thinking skills" (Sebranek, Meyer, & Kemper, p. 44). Writing-to-learn activities can be used to help students reflect on and explore ideas and concepts they are reading about in class, thereby helping students to construct meaning. As with learning log entries, these writing activities are intended to be brief and can be assigned at any point during the class period.

How to use it:

1. Select the concept you want students to explore.

2. Assign the writing-to-learn activity at any time during class, depending upon the topic and your purpose. The suggestions below are grouped into prereading, during reading, and after reading activities. When designing a writing topic, remember that the task should not require students merely to regurgitate facts from the text. Instead, it should ask students to reflect on or apply what they are learning in some way.

3. Assign the topic and give students three to five minutes "think time" to consider their response.

4. Have students write for five minutes on the topic. Remind them that you will be assessing their responses based on the depth of thought shown.

Prereading

-   **Alphabet Soup.** This activity can be used to activate students' prior knowledge. On the first day of a unit, have students work in groups to complete the pre-reading sections of a K-W-L, DR/TA, or PreP worksheet. After the groups have collaborated on the worksheets, each student should spend five minutes writing about their prior knowledge. If the topic is new to most of the students, explain it in brief terms and have the students write for five minutes on any first impressions they have about the subject.

- **Anticipation Guides.** Have students complete a true-false anticipation guide on the subject of the unit. Before they discuss their answers as a class, have students select one of the guide's statements and write for five minutes, defending their answer for that statement.

- **Problematic Situations.** Instead of having students discuss potential solutions to a problematic situation, have each student write his own solution to the problem.

- **Yesterday's News.** Students spend five minutes at the beginning of class writing a note to a student (real or fictional) who missed the previous class. In their note, students explain how one idea from that class (they can select which concept or point to discuss) is particularly important to their lives.

- **One-liners.** At the beginning of class, have students write down, in one sentence, the importance or relevance of something they learned in the previous lesson. Award the writer of the most succinct, accurate, thought-provoking one-liner extra credit.

- **A Rose by Any Other Name.** Creating analogies is a powerful learning tool because it requires students to use complex reasoning skills. At the beginning of class, have students brainstorm a list of terms, concepts, or ideas from the current unit. Write these on the board, and label that list "A." Next, write another list of your own choosing consisting of five or six items students enjoy. Label that list "B." For example, you might list popular video games, professional sports teams, or rock groups. Explain what an analogy is and tell students they are going to write an analogy that identifies the ways in which one of the topics from list A is similar to one of the items on list

155

B. For example, students may have identified the concept of rational numbers for list A. If list B included the Chicago Bears, Green Bay Packers, Denver Broncos, and Miami Dolphins, students would select one of those teams—the Broncos, for example—and write an analogy comparing the attributes of rational numbers to certain characteristics of the Broncos. Once students understand the writing task, give them a few minutes to select an item from list A to compare to one item from list B. Then tell students they have five minutes to write their analogies.

During Class/Reading

- **Crystal Ball.** Stop the lesson at a key juncture, and have students predict in writing what they think will happen next. (This is especially effective with topics that involve a cause and effect relationship or with narrative text.)

- **Fast Food for Thought.** After explaining a particular concept, process, or vocabulary term, have students write a question they still have about that topic. Then have students exchange papers and either answer the writer's question or suggest resources they could use to locate the answer.

- **Out of This World.** At a convenient point during the day's lesson, have students write for ten minutes on the following: You are an alien from another galaxy. Your spacecraft has just landed outside of the school building and your first stop is in our classroom. Write your observations of the lesson, the teacher, and the students in the class.

After the Lesson/Reading

- **Dear Diary.** Ask students to assume the identity of an historic figure who is/was intimately involved in the lesson topic and to write a diary entry as if they were that individual. For example, students studying the Salem Witch Trials might assume the role of someone accused of witchcraft and compose a diary entry chronicling her thoughts at that time.

Reflection Strategies

- **Read All Instructions Before Operating!** Have students write instructions for how to solve a problem or perform a skill they have just learned.

- **The Last Word.** Students spend the last ten minutes of class writing you a letter about something they do not understand or need help with in the current unit. In addition to revealing to students what they do not know, this writing task can inform you about what needs to be reviewed or clarified during the next lesson.

- **"And the winner is..."** This activity works best at the end of a unit as it is a student-led form of review. Have students brainstorm on the following: The publisher of the textbook we use wants student input on the content of the chapter we are studying. Specifically, they want to know which individual or concept included in this chapter/unit has had the greatest impact on your life and why. Once students have had an opportunity to consider the possibilities, have each student write a letter to the publisher identifying his/her choice and citing specific reasons for the nomination. Nominations will be considered on the basis of the persuasiveness of each argument.

Reflection Strategies

38. Creative Debate

What is it?

The creative debate strategy promotes debate, creative thinking, and thinking from different perspectives. Students debate a topic from a character's point of view.

How to use it:

1. Divide the class into thirds. Have one third of the class turn their chairs to face another third of the class for debate. The other class members are observers. An alternative strategy is to have observers collect data for students involved in the debate. Effective debate criteria are established in advance with all students.

2. Decide on a relevant topic to discuss. Clearly define the topic and outcome (e.g., fighting in the Korean war, or bombing Pearl Harbor).

3. Ask row 1 to take a position in support of the topic and row 2 to take the opposite point of view.

4. Each student selects a character from the past or present who supports the position the student has taken, either for or against the issue. The student debates the topic from that character's point of view and may take on the character's mannerisms, posture, or voice.

5. Have each student involved in the debate introduce him or herself as the character to the rest of the class.

6. The student does not have to agree with the viewpoint he is asked to represent.

7. Students debate from their character's point of view for ten minutes. Reverse roles if appropriate, or have one row of students become the observers and the observers take a position. Debate for another five to ten minutes.

McREL

8. Process the activity. Have the observers share the data they collected. Reflective questions might include, "How difficult was it to share information from a different perspective? Why was it difficult and what did you learn? What might you do differently next time?"

Reflection Strategies

39. Discussion Web

What is it?

The Discussion Web gives all students an opportunity to assume responsibility and share their own ideas in discussion, not just the verbally talented students. It is tailored after McTighe and Lyman's (1988) think-pair-share discussion cycle. In the Discussion Web, all students think individually about the items they want to share in the discussion and then share their ideas with a partner. This private "think time" promotes total class involvement and honors the wait time necessary for developing insightful thoughts to share. Student accountability is also included by having students share their thinking with each other. The Discussion Web incorporates all four areas of language arts: listening, speaking, reading, and writing. It can be used anytime during the learning process—as a prereading activity, a prewriting activity, a postreading strategy, or to help students organize their ideas while reading a selection.

How to use it:

1. Prepare students for reading the selection: activate their background knowledge, introduce new vocabulary words, and explain the purpose for reading. For example, students are going to read *Jack and the Beanstalk*. To pull forward prior knowledge, ask the students, "What characteristics might make a person do mean things?" Then discuss their thoughts. Introduce any difficult vocabulary words during this discussion so the words are used within the context of the story being read. Explain that the purpose of reading the story is to determine if it was all right for Jack to take the things from the giant's castle. Students will construct support for both positions.

2. Have the students read both versions of *Jack and the Beanstalk*.

3. Introduce the Discussion Web with the questions, "Was it all right for Jack to take things from the giant's castle?" written in the middle. Explain to the students that they will have to

construct support for both viewpoints by citing specific reasons. Give each student wait time to construct his own reasons for each viewpoint. Encourage students to write one or two ideas down; this ensures participation by all.

4. Pair each student with a partner to share their written ideas. Ask them to continue to discuss reasons for each viewpoint and to take turns writing down in the Yes/No column the reason why they think it is or is not all right for Jack to take from the giant. Give them five to ten minutes to write their reasons.

5. Pair one set of students with another set of partners. Ask the group of four students to compare their Yes/No reasons. Once students have compared notes and added any new ideas to their web, they form a conclusion to share with the class. They decide if Jack was justified in bringing things home from the castle and their major reason for that decision. They write this statement at the bottom of their web under Conclusion. One person is selected to share the group's conclusion with the rest of the class.

6. Call on each spokesperson to report for their groups as part of the whole class discussion. After each person has shared their group's conclusion, the discussion can be opened up for further discussion by all members. The teacher monitors for effective discussion skills.

7. As a follow-up activity, have the students individually write their own conclusion and their reasons for it on the Discussion Web question section. Also, have the students reflect on the specific discussion skills they used throughout the activity, and their strengths or areas that need improvement. This final writing helps the learners bring closure to the Discussion Web.

Reflection Strategies

Examples of Visual Representations: **Discussion Webs**

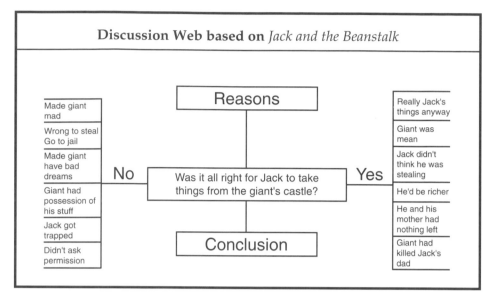

Discussion Web based on *Jack and the Beanstalk*

Reasons

No		Yes
Made giant mad		Really Jack's things anyway
Wrong to steal Go to jail		Giant was mean
Made giant have bad dreams	**Was it all right for Jack to take things from the giant's castle?**	Jack didn't think he was stealing
Giant had possession of his stuff		He'd be richer
Jack got trapped		He and his mother had nothing left
Didn't ask permission		Giant had killed Jack's dad

Conclusion

Note: From "The discussion web: a graphic aid for learning across the curriculum," by D.E. Alvermann, 1991, in *The Reading Teacher, 45* (2), pages 92-99. Copyright © 1991 by the International Reading Association. Reprinted (with slight adaptations) with permission.

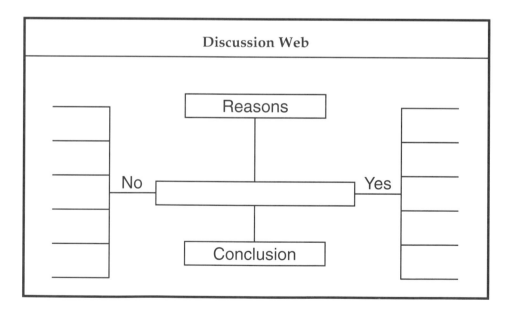

Discussion Web

Reasons

No | Yes

Conclusion

McREL

Reflection Strategies

40. Scored Discussion

What is it?

Scored Discussion gives students the opportunity to practice and to evaluate effective discussion skills. A small group of students carry on a content-related discussion while classmates listen. Meanwhile, the teacher and the rest of the class observe the small group discussion and score individual contributions to the discussion. Students are awarded points for contributing relevant information, using evidence, asking clarifying questions, making analogies, and encouraging other group members to participate. Negative points are assigned for interruptions, irrelevant comments, and personal attacks. At the conclusion, the teacher and observers provide feedback to discussion members about their level of understanding of the content and about the discussion process.

How to use it:

1. Determine the criteria and/or indicators of a successful discussion. Record the criteria on chart paper for reference during discussion.

2. After students finish reading a selection in which the author takes a position on an issue (e.g. Paine, Thoreau, John F. Kennedy, Malcolm X), have them consider the following: What position does the writer of the article take on the issue? Decide how the position agrees or disagrees with your own.

3. Allow all students time to record their arguments and rationale.

4. Select 6-8 students for the small group.

5. Teach the strategy.

   - Explain the criteria.

   - Stress appropriateness rather than quantity, and establish time limits.

   - Allow student observation time to demonstrate objectivity.

Reflection Strategies

- Provide feedback.
- Hold all students accountable.

6. Repeat the strategy after students read additional selections, allowing each student the chance to be in the small group.

Examples of Visual Representations: **Discussion Score Sheet**

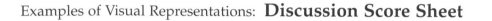

Discussion Score Sheet

Student _____

Class _____

Positive/Productive Behavior	Points
(1) 1. Offers his/her position on a topic	_____ x(1) = _____
(1) 2. Makes a relevant comment	_____ x(1) = _____
(3) 3. Uses evidence to support position	_____ x(3) = _____
(2) 4. Points out contradictions in another person's statements	_____ x(2) = _____
(2) 5. Recognizes when another person makes an irrelevant comment	_____ x(2) = _____
(3) 6. Develops an analogy	_____ x(3) = _____
(1) 7. Asks a clarifying question	_____ x(1) = _____
(3) 8. Uses active listening skills (e.g., rephrases or restates what another student says before commenting)	_____ x(3) = _____

Non-Productive Behavior	Points
(-2) 1. Not paying attention or distracting others	_____ x(-2) = _____
(-2) 2. Interruption	_____ x(-2) = _____
(-1) 3. Irrelevant comment	_____ x(-1) = _____
(-3) 4. Monopolizing	_____ x(-3) = _____
(-3) 5. Personal attack	_____ x(-3) = _____

Total Points:

Positive/Productive Behavior: _____

Non-Productive Behavior: _ _____

Overall Total: _____

Grade: _____

Adapted from Fred Newmann, University of Wisconsin

Bibliography

Bibliography

Alvermann, D.E. (1991). The discussion web: A graphic aid for learning across the curriculum. *The Reading Teacher, 45* (2), 92-99.

Alvermann, D.E., Dillon, D.R., & O'Brien, D.G. (1988). *Using discussion to promote reading comprehension.* Newark, DE: International Reading Association.

Anderson, C.W., & Smith, E.L. (1984). Children's preconceptions and content area textbooks. In G. Duffy, L. Roehler, and J. Mason (Eds.), *Comprehension instruction: Perspectives and suggestions* (pp. 187-201). New York: Longman.

Anderson, R.C. (1984). Role of reader's schema in comprehension, learning and memory. In R.C. Anderson, J. Osborn, & R.J. Tierney (Eds.), *Learning to read in American schools: Basal readers and content texts* (pp. 243-258). Hillsdale, NJ: Erlbaum.

Anderson, R.C., & Biddle W.B. (1975). On asking people about what they do when they are reading. In G. Bower (Ed.), *Psychology of learning and motivation*. New York: Academic Press.

Anderson, R.C., Hiebert, E.H., Scott, J.A., & Wilkinson, I.A.G. (1985). *Becoming a nation of readers: The report of the Commission on Reading.* Washington, DC: National Institute of Education.

Anderson, T.H., & Armbruster, B.B. (1984). Content area textbooks. In R.C. Anderson, J. Osborn, & R.J. Tierney (Eds.), *Learning to read in American schools: Basal readers and content texts* (pp. 193-226). Hillsdale, NJ: Erlbaum.

Anthony, H.M., and Raphael, T. E. (1989). Using questioning strategies to promote students' active comprehension of content area material. In D. Lapp, J. Flood, & N. Farnan (Eds.), *Content area reading and learning: Instructional strategies.* Englewood Cliffs, NJ: Prentiss-Hall.

Armbruster, B. (1992). Content reading in RT: The last two decades. *The Reading Teacher, 46* (2), 166-167.

Armbruster, B.B., & Nagy, W.E. (1992). Vocabulary in content area lessons. *The Reading Teacher, 45* (7), 550-551.

Baker, L. (1985). How do we know when we don't understand? Standards for evaluating text comprehension. In D.L. Forrest-Pressley, G.E. MacKinnon, & T.G. Waller (Eds.), *Metacognition, cognition, and human performance* (pp. 155-205). New York: Academic Press.

Baker, L., & Brown, A.L. (1984). Cognitive monitoring in reading. In J. Flood (Ed.), *Understanding reading comprehension.* Newark, DE: International Reading Association.

Baldwin, R.S., Ford, J.C., & Readance, J.E. (1981). Teaching word connotations: An alternative strategy. *Reading World*, 21, 103-108.

Barton, M.L. (1997, March). Addressing the literacy crisis: Teaching reading in the content areas. NASSP *Bulletin, 81* (587), 22-30.

Bibliography

Beck, I., & McKeown, M. (1981). Developing questions that promote comprehension: The story map. *Language Arts* (November/December), 913-918.

Bransford, J.D., Sherwood, R., Vye, N., & Rieser, J. (1986). Teaching thinking and problem solving. *American Psychologist, 41,* 1078-1089.

Braselton, S. & Decker, B. (1994, November). Using graphic organizers to improve the reading of mathematics. *The Reading Teacher, 48*(3), 276-281.

Brophy, J. (1992) Probing the subtleties of subject-matter teaching. *Educational Leadership, 49* (7), 4-8.

Brown, A.L. (1982). Learning how to learn from reading. In J.A. Langer & M.T. Smith-Burke (Eds.), *Reader meets author/bridging the gap* (pp.26-54). Newark, DE: International Reading Association.

Brown, A.L. (1985). *Teaching students to think as they read: Implications for curriculum reform* (Reading Education Report No. 58). Urbana, IL: University of Illinois, The Center for The Study of Reading.

Brown, A.L., Bransford, J.D., Ferrara, R.A., & Campione, J.S. (1983). Learning, remembering, and understanding. In J.H. Flavell & E. M. Markham (Eds.), *Handbook of Child Psychology* (Vol. 3). New York: Wiley.

Brown, A.L., Day, J.D., & Jones, R. (1983). The development of plans for summarizing texts. *Child Development, 54,* 968-979.

Brown, J.E., Phillips, L.B., & Stephens, E.C. (1993). *Toward literacy: Theory and applications for teaching writing in the content areas.* Belmont, CA: Wadsworth.

Bruner, J.S. (1971). *Toward a theory of instruction.* New York: Norton.

Buehl, D. (1995). *Classroom strategies for interactive learning* (Monograph of the Wisconsin State Reading Association). Schofield, WI: Wisconsin State Reading Association.

Caverly, D.C., Mandeville, T. F., & Nicholson, S. A. (November 1995). PLAN: A study-reading strategy for informational text. *Journal of Adolescent & Adult Literacy, 39*(3), 190-199.

Campbell, J.R., Voelkl, K.E., and Donahue, P.L. (1997, August). Report in brief: NAEP 1996 trends in academic progress. [On-line database]. Washington, DC: National Center for Education Statistics. http://www.ed.gov/NCES/naep/96report/97986t7.shtml and http://www.ed.gov/NCES/naep/96report/97986t8.shtml

Cook, D. (Ed.). (1986). *A guide for curriculum planning reading.* Madison, WI: Wisconsin Department of Public Instruction.

Costa, A.L. (1991). Toward a model of human intellectual functioning. In A. Costa (Ed.), *Developing minds: A resource book for teaching thinking.* (Rev. ed, pp.62-65). Alexandria, VA: Association for Supervision and Curriculum Development.

McREL

Bibliography

Costa, A.L., & Garmston, R.J. (1994). *Cognitive coaching: A foundation for renaissance schools.* Norwood, MA: Christopher-Gordon.

Cullinan, B. (1987). *Children's literature in the reading program.* Newark, DE: International Reading Association.

Daggett, W. (1990, November). *Quality in education: A new collaborative initiative and process for change.* Seminar presented in Linden, MI.

Davey, B. (1983). Think aloud: Modeling the cognitive processes of reading comprehension. *Journal of Reading, 27* (1), 44-47.

Dole, J., Duffy, G., Roehler, L., & Pearson, P.D. (1991). Moving from the old to the new: Research on reading comprehension instruction. *Review of Educational Research, 61,* 239-264.

Dupuis, M.M., & Merchant, L.H. (Eds.). (1993). *Reading across the curriculum.* Bloomington, IN: ERIC Clearinghouse on Reading and Communication Skills.

Feathers, L.M. (1993). *Infotext: Reading and learning.* Markham, Ontario, Canada: Pippin.

Fowler, G.L. (1982). Developing comprehension skills in primary students through the use of story frames. *The Reading Teacher, 36* (2), 176-179.

Frager, A.M. (1993). Affective dimensions of content area reading. *Journal of Reading, 36* (8), 616-622.

Frayer, D.A., Frederick, W.C., & Klausmeier, H.J. (1969). *A schema for testing the level of concept mastery* (Technical Report No. 16). Madison, WI: University of Wisconsin Research and Development Center for Cognitive Learning.

Fulwiler, T. (1987). *Teaching with writing.* Portsmouth, NH: Boynton/Cook.

Gagné, R.M. (1970). *Conditions of learning.* New York: Holt, Rinehart and Winston.

Garner, R. (1987). *Metacognition and reading comprehension.* Norwood, NJ: Ablex.

Gavelek, J. R. & Raphael, T. E. (1985). Metacognition, instruction, and the role of questioning activities. In D.L. Forrest-Pressley, G.E. MacKinnon, and T. G. Waller (Eds.), *Metacognition, cognition, and human performance, Vol. 2.* pp. 103-106. NY: Academic Press, Inc.

Gillett, J. W., & Temple, C. (1983). *Understanding reading problems: Assessment and instruction.* Boston: Little, Brown.

Haggard, M.R. (1982, December). The vocabulary self-collection strategy: An active approach to word learning. *Journal Reading, 26* (3), 203-207.

Healy, J.M. (1990). *Endangered minds: Why our children don't think.* New York: Simon and Schuster.

Heimlich, J.E., & Pittelman, S.D. (1986). *Semantic mapping classrooms applications.* Newark, DE: International Reading Association.

Bibliography

Herber, H. (1978). *Teaching reading in content areas.* (2nd ed.). Englewood Cliffs, NJ: Prentice-Hall.

Herrmann, B.A., (Ed.). (1994). *The volunteer tutor's toolbox.* Newark, DE: International Reading Association.

Jenkins, J. (1974). Remember that old theory of memory? Well forget it! *American Psychologist, 29,* 785-795.

Johnson, B.E. (1992). Concept question chain: A framework for thinking and learning about text. *Reading Horizons, 32* (4), 263-278.

Johnson, D.D. & Pearson, P.D. (1984). *Teaching reading vocabulary.* (2nd ed.). New York: Holt, Rinehart and Winston.

Johnson, D.W., John, R.T., Holubec, E.J., & Roy, P. (1984). *Circles of learning.* Alexandria, VA: Association for Supervision and Curriculum Development.

Jones, B.F., Palinscar, A.S., Ogle, D.S. & Carr, E.G. (1987). *Strategic teaching and learning: Cognitive instruction in the content areas.* Alexandria, VA, and Elmhurst, IL: Association for Supervision and Curriculum Development and North Central Regional Educational Laboratory.

Kätz, K., & Kätz, C. (1991). *Reading strategies for the primary grades.* Bloomington, IN: EDINFO Press.

Kintsch, W. (1974). *The representation of meaning in memory.* Hillsdale, NJ: Lawrence Erlbaum.

Laflamme, J.G. (1997). The effect of the Multiple Exposure Vocabulary Method and the Target Reading/Writing Strategy on test scores. *Journal of Adolescent and Adult Literacy, 40* (5), 372-381.

Langer, L.A. (1981, November). From theory to practice: A prereading plan. *Journal of Reading, 25,* 152-156.

Manna, A.L., Misheff, S. (1987, November). What teachers say about their own reading development. *Journal of reading, 31* (2), 160-168.

Marzano, R.J. (1991). *Cultivating thinking in English and the language arts.* Urbana, IL: National Council of Teachers of English.

Marzano, R.J. (1992). *A different kind of classroom: Teaching with dimensions of learning.* Alexandria, VA: Association for Supervision and Curriculum Development.

Marzano, R.J., & Pickering, D.J., with Arredondo, D.E., Blackburn, G.J., Brandt, R.S., Moffett, C.A., Paynter, D.E., & Whisler, J.S. (1997). *Dimensions of Learning* (2nd ed.) . Alexandria, VA: Association for Supervision and Curriculum Development.

McCombs, B.L. and Barton, M.L. (October, 1998). Motivating secondary students to read their textbooks. NASSP *Bulletin, 82* (600), 24-33.

Bibliography

McGowen, C.S. (1990). *Remedial reading for elementary school students.* Bloomington, IN: ERIC Clearinghouse on Reading and Communication Skills.

McTighe, J. (1986). Thinking about adolescent thinking. *The Early Adolescence Magazine, 1*(1) 7-13.

McTighe, J., & Lyman, F.T. (1988). Cueing thinking in the classroom: The promise of theory-embedded tools. *Educational Leadership, 45* (7), 18-24.

Miller, W. H. (1997). *Reading & writing remediation kit: Ready-to-use strategies and activities to build content reading and writing skills.* West Nyack, NY: The Center for Applied Research in Education.

Moore, D.W., Readance, J.E., & Rickelman, R.J. (1982). *Prereading activities for content area reading and learning.* Newark, DE: International Reading Association.

Moore, D.W., Readance, J.E., & Rickelman, R.J. (1982). A historical explanation of content area reading instruction. *Reading Research Quarterly, 18,* 419-438.

Moss, B. (1991). Children's nonfiction trade books: A complement to content area texts. *The Reading Teacher, 45,* 26-32.

National Assessment of Educational Progress. (1985). *The reading report card.* (Report No. 15-R01). Princeton, NJ: Educational Testing Service.

Ogle, D. (1986, February). The K-W-L: A teaching model that develops active reading of expository text. *The Reading Teacher, 45* (4), 298-306.

Ogle, D.M. (1989). The know, want to know, learning strategy. In K.D. Muth (Ed.), *Children's comprehension of text* (pp. 205-223). Newark, DE: International Reading Association.

Olson, M.W., and Gee, T.C. (1991). Content reading instruction in the primary grades: Perceptions and strategies. *The Reading Teacher, 45*(4), 298-306.

Osman, M.E. & Hannafin, M. J. (1992). Metacognition research and theory: Analysis and implications for instructional design. *Educational Technology Research and Development, 40*(2), 83-89.

Palinscar, A.S., & Brown, A.L. (1985). Reciprocal teaching: Activities to promote "reading with your mind." In T.L. Harris & E.J. Cooper (Eds.), *Reading, thinking, and concept development* (pp. 147-158). New York: College Board Publications.

Paul, R. (Ed.). (1990). *Critical thinking: What every person needs to survive in a rapidly changing world.* Rohnert Park, CA: Center for Critical Thinking and Moral Critique.

Pearson, P.D. (1985). *The comprehension revolution: A twenty-year history of process and practice related to reading comprehension* (Reading Education Report No. 57). Urbana, IL: University of Illinois, The Center for the Study of Reading.

Perkins, D. (1993, October). Teaching & learning for understanding. *NJEA Review,* 10-17.

Bibliography

Pogrow, S. (1993, May 26). The forgotten question in the Chapter I debate: Why are the students having so much trouble learning? *Education Week, 26,* 36.

Pope., J., & Lilly, K. (1988). *Animals.* New York: Lothrop, Lee and Shepard.

Raphael, T. E. (1982). Question-answering strategies for children. *The Reading Teacher, 36,* 186-190.

Raphael, T. E. (1986). Teaching question-answer relationships, revisited. *The Reading Teacher, 39,* 516-522.

Raphael, T.E., Kirschner, B.W., & Engelert, C.S. (1988). Expository writing program: Making connections between reading and writing. *The Reading Teacher, 41,* 790-795.

Resnick, L.B. (1987). *Education and learning to think.* Washington, DC: National Academy Press.

Resnick, L.B. (1984). Cognitive science as educational research: Why we need it now. In National Academy of Education, *Improving Education: Perspectives on Educational Research* (pp. 181-205). Pittsburgh, PA: University of Pittsburgh, Learning Research and Development Center.

Richardson, J.S., & Morgan, R.F. (1994). *Reading to learn in the content areas.* Belmont, CA: Wadsworth.

Robinson, F. (1961). *Effective study.* New York: Harper and Row.

Rosenblatt, L.M. (1967). *Literature as exploration.* New York: Noble & Noble.

Routman, R. (1991). *Invitations: Changing as teachers and learners K-12.* Portsmouth, NH: Heinemann.

Rowe, M.B. (1974). Wait time and rewards as instructional variables: Their influences on language, logic, and fate control. *Journal of Research in Science and Teaching, 11,* 81-94.

Santa, C.M. (1988). *Content reading including study systems.* Dubuque, IA: Kendall/Hunt.

Santa, C.M., & Alvermann, D.E. (Eds.). (1991). *Science learning: Processes and applications.* Newark, DE: International Reading Association.

Schwartz, R. (1988, November). Learning to learn vocabulary in content area textbooks. *Journal of Reading, 32,* 108-117.

Schwartz, R., & Raphael, T. (1985, November). Concept definition: A key to improving students' vocabulary. *The Reading Teacher, 39*(2), 676-682.

Sebranek, P., Meyer. V., & Kemper, D. (1996). *A teacher's guide to accompany Writers Inc.* Wilmington, MA: Write Source.

Smith, P., & Tompkins, G. (1988, October). Structured notetaking: A new strategy for content area readers. *Journal of Reading, 32*(1), 46-53.

Bibliography

Sorgen, M., & Wolfe, P. (1998). *Strengthening student learning by applying the latest research on the brain to your classroom teaching.* Bellevue, WA: Bureau of Education & Research.

Stauffer, R.G. (1969). *Developing reading maturity as a cognitive process.* New York: Harper & Row.

Stauffer, R. G. (1969). *Directing reading maturity as a cognitive process.* New York: Harper & Row.

Stedman, L. C., & Kaestle, C.F. (1991). Literacy and reading performance in the United States from 1880 to the present. In C. F. Kaestle, H. Damon-Moore, L.C. Stedman, K. Tinsley, & W. V. Trollinger (Eds.), *Literacy in the United States: Readers and reading since 1880* (pp. 75-128). New Haven, CT: Yale University Press.

Strenberg, R.J. (1987). Teaching critical thinking: Eight easy ways to fail before you begin. *Phi Delta Kappan, 68,* 456-459.

Thiessen, D., & Matthias, M. (Eds.). (1993). *The wonderful world of mathematics: A critically annotated list of children's books in mathematics.* Reston, VA: National Council of Teachers of Mathematics.

Tompkins, G.E. (1994). *Teaching writing: Balancing process and product* (2nd ed.). New York: MacMillan College Publishing Co., Inc.

Vacca, R.T., & Vacca, J.L. (1993). *Content area reading* (4th ed.). New York: Harper Collins.

van Dijk, T.A. (1980). *Macrostructures.* Hillsdale, NJ: Lawrence Erlbaum.

Vygotsky, L.S. (1978). *Mind and society: The development of higher mental processes.* Cambridge, MA: Harvard University Press.

Wolfe, P., & Sorgen, M. (1990). *Mind, memory and learning,* handout. (Unpublished).

Wood, K. (1988). Guiding students through informational text. *The Reading Teacher, 41* (9), 912-920.

Wood, K.D., Lapp, D., & Flood, J. (1992). *Guiding readers through text: A review of study guides.* Newark, DE: International Reading Association.

Wood, K.D., & Muth, K.D. (1991). The case for improved instruction in the middle grades. *Journal of Reading, 35* (2), 84-90.

Zarnowski, M., & Gallagher, A.F. (Eds.). (1993). *Children's literature & social studies: Selecting and using notable books in the classroom.* Washington, DC: National Council for the Social Studies.

About the Authors

Internationally known educational/business consultant Rachel Ann Billmeyer has extensive experience putting educational theory into practice. Dr. Billmeyer has taught at elementary, secondary and university levels, and worked with renowned educational researchers. She has served in leadership positions, including as Director of Staff Development and Instruction for a nationally recognized school district, member of the Nebraska Association of Supervision and Curriculum Development (ASCD) Board, and Program Chair for the Midwest ASCD Regional Conference. Dr. Billmeyer has conducted training sessions in Reading in the Content Areas, Dimensions of Learning, Performance-Based Assessment, Cognitive Coaching, Creating Fine-Tuned Teams, and New Teacher/Mentor Programs. She was the 1993 recipient of the Nebraska Literacy Award, and is author of *A Growing Curriculum.*

A senior associate at McREL, Mary Lee Barton has provided technical assistance and training to teachers, curriculum developers, and school administrators nationally in the areas of content area reading instruction, writing across the curriculum, and complex reasoning skills. She brings a wealth of practical experience to her workshops; prior to joining McREL, Barton taught English, developmental reading, and communication skills for 12 years at the middle school and high school levels. She earned her master's degree in adult continuing education with a focus on staff development. In addition to training and consulting, Barton writes extensively on issues in education. She is the lead author of *Helping Students Acquire and Integrate Knowledge: A Facilitator's Guide,* which she wrote with Dr. Robert Marzano for an ASCD video series. Barton is author of "Addressing the Literacy Crisis: Teaching Reading in the Content Areas" and is co- author with Dr. Barbara McCombs of "Motivating Secondary School Students to Read their Textbooks," both published in the National Association of Secondary School Principals *Bulletin.*